Digha ❦ Lodge

A Short History of the Jamil Family

SYED SABIR JAMIL

iUniverse, Inc.
Bloomington

Digha Lodge
A Short History of the Jamil Family

Copyright © 2012 Syed Sabir Jamil

iUniverse books may be ordered through booksellers or by contacting:

iUniverse
1663 Liberty Drive
Bloomington, IN 47403
www.iuniverse.com
1-800-Authors (1-800-288-4677)

ISBN: 978-1-4697-8610-0 (sc)
ISBN: 978-1-4697-8609-4 (hc)
ISBN: 978-1-4697-8611-7 (e)

Library of Congress Control Number: 2012903398

Printed in the United States of America

iUniverse rev. date: 3/12/2012

Illustrations by Seong Eun Roelle Kim
Pictures edited by Tariq M Sajjad

Together in Silence ... Forever!

For

Ayesha Jamil
Mahroo Shahbaz
Rida Waheed
Sundas Ali
Muniba Tariq
Maryam Tariq

&

Syed Sabih Nasir
Syed Abdullah Nasir
Syed Aashir Waheed
Asad Ali Azam
Arsalan Ali
Faiz Bin Khalid
Zaid Bin Khalid

&

others
who might be
on the way!

The Jamil Family Tree

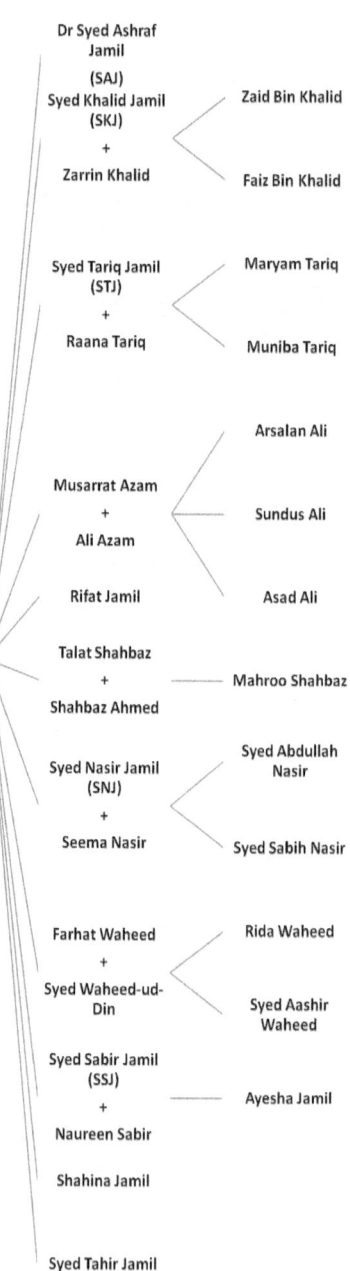

Syed Zahoorul Haque
(Grandfather)

+

Majidun Nisa
(Grandmother)

Sayed Jamil Ahmad
(Father)

+

Hafeez-un-Nisa
(Mother)

Akhter Hussain
(See Chart B)

Zafirul Haque
(See Chart B)

Roqaiya Khatoon
(See Chart B)

Abdus Shakoor
(See Chart B)

Dr Syed Ashraf Jamil
(SAJ)

Syed Khalid Jamil
(SKJ)

+

Zarrin Khalid

Zaid Bin Khalid

Faiz Bin Khalid

Syed Tariq Jamil
(STJ)

+

Raana Tariq

Maryam Tariq

Muniba Tariq

Musarrat Azam

+

Ali Azam

Arsalan Ali

Sundus Ali

Asad Ali

Rifat Jamil

Talat Shahbaz

+

Shahbaz Ahmed

Mahroo Shahbaz

Syed Nasir Jamil
(SNJ)

+

Seema Nasir

Syed Abdullah Nasir

Syed Sabih Nasir

Farhat Waheed

+

Syed Waheed-ud-Din

Rida Waheed

Syed Aashir Waheed

Syed Sabir Jamil
(SSJ)

+

Naureen Sabir

Ayesha Jamil

Shahina Jamil

Syed Tahir Jamil

The Jamil Family Tree

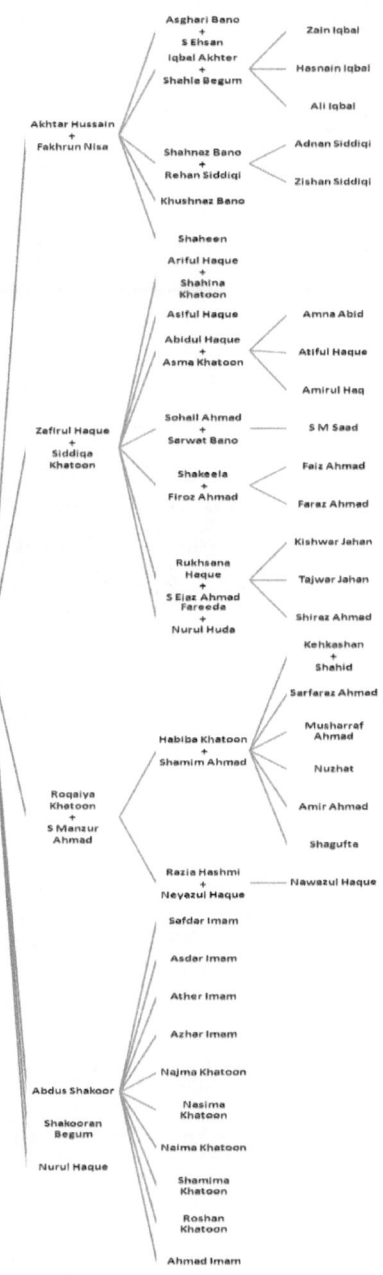

FATHER'S
brothers & sisters
& their children

Akhtar Hussain
+
Fakhrun Nisa

Asghari Bano
+
S Ehsan

Iqbal Akhter
+
Shahla Begum

Zain Iqbal

Hasnain Iqbal

Ali Iqbal

Shahnaz Bano
+
Rehan Siddiqi

Adnan Siddiqi

Zishan Siddiqi

Khushnaz Bano

Shaheen

Ariful Haque
+
Shahina
Khatoon

Asiful Haque

Abidul Haque
+
Asma Khatoon

Amna Abid

Atiful Haque

Amirul Haq

Zafirul Haque
+
Siddiqa
Khatoon

Sohail Ahmad
+
Sarwat Bano

S M Saad

Shakeela
+
Firoz Ahmad

Faiz Ahmad

Faraz Ahmad

Rukhsana
Haque
+
S Ejaz Ahmad

Kishwar Jahan

Tajwar Jahan

Shiraz Ahmad

Fareeda
+
Nurul Huda

Kehkashan
+
Shahid

Sarfaraz Ahmad

Roqaiya
Khatoon
+
S Manzur
Ahmad

Habiba Khatoon
+
Shamim Ahmad

Musharraf
Ahmad

Nuzhat

Amir Ahmad

Shagufta

Razia Hashmi
+
Neyazul Haque

Nawazul Haque

Abdus Shakoor

Shakooran
Begum

Nurul Haque

Safdar Imam

Asdar Imam

Ather Imam

Azhar Imam

Najma Khatoon

Nasima
Khatoon

Naima Khatoon

Shamima
Khatoon

Roshan
Khatoon

Ahmad Imam

My very special thanks to
Syed Tariq Jamil (STJ),
my elder brother,
for making this possible.

◊ Contents

Preface

THE IDEA TO DOCUMENT THE HISTORY of the Jamil family struck me in November 2002. The principal motivators had been STJ and SKJ, my elder brothers, who, despite my lack of experience and overwhelming lethargy, kept telling me that I could do it.

Recalling the early days, however, has never been an easy or simple undertaking. With an elusive memory like mine, it has always been a difficult endeavor, yet it was still an exercise in soul-searching and stirring enlightenment.

I must thank my parents and my brothers and sisters, for this account would not have been possible without their endless support and encouragement.

I am particularly grateful to STJ for his generous help in verifying the historical validity of the many events and incidents to which I was not an eyewitness but which were nonetheless very momentous and worth recording.

I must also thank Robin Barker, my coworker at the Starlet Academy, who was kind enough to read the manuscript with a lot of devotion. I am grateful to her for her valuable suggestions.

I expect this book to serve as an entertaining journal for the next generation of kids, who, I believe, have every right to know how their ancestors, relatives, and relations faced and overcame the challenges of life. Family members, I hope, will be able to identify with the people I have tried to portray most faithfully.

But this book is also for those who are always in search of stories from Asia, particularly the culturally rich Indo-Pak subcontinent.

I have deliberately kept the language plain and simple so that the book serves its purpose in the best possible manner.

Father

OUR FATHER, SAYED JAMIL AHMAD DIGHVI, was born in P.S. Islampur, District Patna of Bihar province, India. It was July 10, 1922, as per date of birth recorded in his matriculation certificate. His father, Syed Zahoorul Haque, was an employee in the survey department of the government of Bihar; he departed soon after his retirement from public service, leaving behind our *daadi* (grandmother), Mrs. Majidun Nisa; father's two elder brothers, Syed Akhtar Hussain and Syed Zafirul Haque; and their elder sister, Roqaiya Khatoon; along with our father.

After the death of her husband, *daadi* moved to her ancestral home in Digha (Nawab Kothi) in District Patna. As soon as she got there, she sent her eldest son, Syed Akhtar Hussain, to Calcutta, where he was admitted to the Calcutta Muslim Orphanage. Then she sent Syed Zafirul Haq to Ranchi, where he was admitted to the Ranchi Zilla School. Roqaiya Khatoon and Sayed Jamil Ahmad stayed back in Digha in the guardianship of our father's maternal uncle, Mohammad Osmanul Haque.

In Digha, Father was admitted to a *madrassa*, a religious school, where he learned the Holy Quran, Urdu, and elementary arithmetic. Later, he joined Class IV of Baladeva English High School, Dinapur Cantonment. The school was situated about three miles from Digha, so Father had to walk the entire distance twice a day, six days a week.

When Father was in Class VIII, Syed Akhtar Hussain, his eldest brother, who was now teaching at the Calcutta Muslim Orphanage, started sending a portion of his income back home for maintenance. This greatly helped *daadi* make ends meet, although living in Digha was not very expensive at that time.

What Better Company Than the Quaid!

In 1938, the annual session of All-India Muslim League was held in Patna Lawn. Father was one of the young men fortunate enough to attend the historic meeting. It provided him with an excellent opportunity to listen to the great Quaid-i-Azam Muhammad Ali Jinnah, the president of the Muslim League, who would go on to become the Father of the Nation.

Father always took pride in the fact that he was able to get so close to that one-of-a-kind, charismatic leader of the subcontinent. "It was in that extraordinary session that the Quaid, after concluding his spellbinding speech in English, also spoke a few words in Urdu: *'Ab Muslim League bohut mazboot ho gia hai'* (Muslim League has now become very strong)." These remarkable words injected new vigor into the participants of the meeting, including Father. Moreover, it was in this very session that Mr. Jinnah was given the title of "Quaid-i-Azam" (The Great Leader).

The Trip to Calcutta, World War II, Public Service, the Dawn of Freedom

When Father was in Class IX, his sister, Roqaiya Khatoon, married Syed Manzoor Ahmad, son of Syed Qamaruddin Ahmad of Neora, District Patna. The same year—1939—Father took the matriculation exam of the Patna University. While filling out the exam form, he for the first time added "Dighvi" ("Resident of Digha") to his name, which became his new last name and remained so for many years thereafter.

In the second quarter of 1939, Father traveled to Calcutta and stayed there for some time with his eldest brother, Syed Akhtar Hussain. Upon return, he received the good news of his passing the matriculation exam. That gave Father new energy and confidence to carry on his studies. Soon after, he joined a local commercial institute where technical subjects were also taught.

In September, the world took a turn for the worse. The Second World War got off to a horrifying start. The heat of its flames was felt all over the world, including in India. In Calcutta, as elsewhere in the world, the cost of living skyrocketed, and rationing was imposed for the first time.

Toward the end of 1940, Father passed the Recruitment Exam held by the Public Service Commission (PSC) of Bengal for appointment of ministerial staff in government offices. A year later, Father was appointed to a permanent position in the legislative department. Subsequently, he took the PSC exams held in 1945, 1948, and 1960, all of which he passed. As a result, he was elevated to the post of section officer in the Ministry of Defence. Prior to this, Father had served as a government officer for about two years in Darjeeling, the summer capital of Bengal. The place was famous for Tiger Hill, about eighty thousand kilometers above sea level. It was known as one of the world's best sites for viewing the sunrise. During his posting there, Father visited the hill station twice to observe the spectacular dawn of the morning sun. The great eastern Himalayan mountains as well as Mount Everest could also be viewed from that terrific spot.

Elsewhere, the ground situation was fast changing as the struggle for freedom from the British Raj was gaining momentum. After the publication of Motilal Nehru's report, it had become clear that the Hindus were not willing to give any rights to the Muslims of India. The Muslims, therefore, kept up their own struggle for independence. Consequently, All-India Muslim League met in Lahore in 1940 under the leadership of Mr. Jinnah and adopted the historic Lahore Resolution (later known as the Pakistan Resolution) calling for the establishment of a separate homeland for the Muslims of India. The plan envisaged the whole of North-West Frontier Province, Baluchistan, Sindh, and the

Punjab on the west, and the whole of Assam and Bengal on the east of India to be called "Pakistan."

It was the Second World War, in fact, that had broken the back of the British government. They quickly realized that they had no option but to transfer power to the rightful owners of the land. Consequently, they started sending various commissions and missions to India, but without any specific roadmap. However, on June 3, 1947, Lord Mountbatten, the last viceroy of India, came up with a definite partition plan to divide the subcontinent into two separate, independent, and sovereign states, Pakistan and India. Thus, two new countries emerged on the map of the world on August 14 and 15, 1947, respectively.

Following the partition, the employees of the central government of India were given two options: continue serving India or migrate to Pakistan. Father opted for Pakistan, and his services were placed at the disposal of the government of East Bengal, which at that time was a province of the newborn Islamic republic.

Interestingly, a day before the official announcement of independence, Father had already left Calcutta for Dacca, the capital of the new province of East Bengal, where he and his colleagues, with blissful hearts and gleaming faces, celebrated the first day of independence. History was made! The rising sun of August 14, 1947, had brought for the residents of the newly created state the first refreshing rays of freedom.

More Exams and Tests

Toward the end of November 1947, Father traveled to Digha to appear in the Senior Cambridge Examination of St. Michael High School, Kurji, Patna, as a private candidate. His subjects included English language, English literature, European literature, European history, vernacular, mathematics, and bookkeeping. As soon as the exam was over, Father found himself faced with another challenge: marriage! His mother wanted him to get married without further delay, for now he was well settled as a government officer. Father accepted her command with all his heart, and the marriage took place on December 22, 1947. His wife, our mother, Hafeezun Nisa, is the youngest daughter of Abdul Rashid of Sharfuddinpur, Balipura. They were happily settled near Manair Sharif of district Patna, Bihar.

In 1948, Father went on a short leave to Digha and brought his wife and mother back to Dacca, where he rented a house not far from his office. In a little while, however, he realized that the house he had rented was neither safe nor comfortable, particularly during rains, so he sent his wife and mother back to Digha.

A year later, Father appeared in the Recruitment Examination of the Public Service Commission (PSC), which he passed, and toward the end of the year, he was promoted and transferred to PSC.

With the new promotion came the luxury of government accommodation in the Azimpur Housing Estate. It was a comfortable flat in all respects with modern facilities, which prompted Father to travel to Digha and bring back his wife and mother. Until 1952, there were no travel restrictions between Pakistan and India; a passport was not required, either.

Merrily settled, Father resumed his academic pursuits after a break of ten years; he enrolled himself in the evening classes of the First Year Intermediate (Arts) at Salimullah Imperial College, Dacca, affiliated with the University of Dacca (now University of Dhaka). He passed the final examination in the First Division, which won him a hefty stipend and motivated him to enroll in the BA classes at the Jagannath College, Dacca. Since the BA classes were held in the evening, Father was able to continue both his work and studies.

The First Joy and More

On May 8, 1952, at five thirty in the evening, when Father returned from work, he found his mother a little upset and worried. Inquiry revealed that his wife had given birth to a baby boy. But why was that a source of concern for his mother? A deeper investigation unveiled that the circumstances in which the child was delivered were very unusual: there was no one in the house except *daadi*, and the neighbors were all taking afternoon naps or away at work. Add to this the fact that there was no telephone service at home. Not knowing what to do in that emergency, *daadi* had banged the door of their next-door neighbors, an English family. Mrs. Field, the lady of the house, was kind enough to help with the delivery. The child was named Syed Ashraf Jamil.

The birth of the first child proved to be a good omen for Father, for in December the same year, Father was selected for a position in the Foreign Service, and on January 2, 1953, he joined the Ministry of External Affairs, Government of Pakistan. Since the offices of the ministry were located in Clifton, Karachi, Father decided to move to his cousin's house, close to his new workplace. His cousin, Muhammad Nezamul Haque, son of Dr. Muhammad Sadrul Haque, was glad to have him.

Those were not the best of times. Living conditions were far from satisfactory, and it adversely affected Father's health. Moreover, Pakistan—being only six years old at the time—was faced with financial stringency. As a result, overseas postings were suspended for an indefinite period and the few officers posted abroad were called back.

Tremors of this traumatic situation were also felt by Father. For instance, his application for an official residence was turned down by the ministry for lack of funds. The denial added salt to his injury and compelled him to revert to his parent organization, the Government of East Pakistan. Thus, after a short stay in Karachi, Father returned to Dacca in July 1953. As later events proved, Father's decision to rejoin the government of East Pakistan was a blessing in disguise: of his unclaimed stipend money lying with Salimullah Imperial College, Father was able to deposit his tuition fees and other dues and appear in the BA final examination. He made the most of the little preparation time he had, exhaustively went through the course books, took the exam, and passed it in the first attempt. He also got a distinction in Urdu language. The other subjects he passed included English, political science, and economics.

Passing the BA exam was considered a great achievement in those days. Given the high standard of education, tough examination, and ruthless grading, it wasn't easy to graduate. With his confidence growing, Father signed up for the LLB course of the Dacca University and successfully completed it. In the meantime, he was able to secure a government flat in the Azimpur Housing Estate, Dacca. It was here that he hired a contractor to build a house in Magh Bazaar, Naya Tola, near Shah Sahib Bari, where he had purchased a piece of land back in 1948. The house was completed in 1957, and soon after, Father and his family moved to Magh Bazaar to live in their own new house.

In 1960, Father was selected by PSC for appointment as Section Officer, a Class 1 Gazetted Post in the East Pakistan Secretariat Service (EPSS). He was placed in the Basic Democracies and Local Government Department. Basic Democracies was a short-lived local government system introduced during the regime of President Ayub Khan in the 1960s. The idea was to set up a grassroots-level democratic system. The political parties active in East Pakistan, however, viewed the new scheme with a lot of skepticism, and some even dubbed it an attempt by the West to grab all power.

Under the new system, Father was appointed as Section Officer-cum-Assistant Commissioner in the Works, Power, and Irrigation (Housing & Planning) Department, Government of East Pakistan. Then, in 1970, his services were placed at the disposal of the Government of West Pakistan. A year later, on January 11, 1971, Father joined the Ministry of Defence, Rawalpindi, as Section Officer.

By that time, seven more children—four boys and three girls—had been added to the family. In February 1971, all of the children, along with their mother, flew from Dacca to Karachi, by PIA, to join Father in Rawalpindi. It was a longer than usual flight, as the plane had to fly via Sri Lanka. India had banned PIA flights over Delhi as a result of the worsening political situation in East Pakistan, for which India was largely to blame.

General Elections and Dirty Politics

In the general elections held toward the end of 1970, the Awami League of Sheikh Mujibur Rehman won the majority of seats in the National Assembly. General Yahya Khan, then president of Pakistan, designated Mujib as the new prime minister of the country. Not respecting the democratic norms, however, the Pakistan People's Party (PPP) of Zulfiqar Ali Bhutto (ZAB) refused to sit in the opposition benches. Also, General Yahya Khan was so obsessed with power that he wanted the new government to retain him as the president. To this Mujib did not agree; he had the right to disagree. However, that allowed Yahya and Bhutto, both hungry for power, to scheme against Mujib and keep him out of the power game. The two did succeed, but only at the cost of the unity of the country.

In fact, the prevailing political hatred was so deep that when a special meeting of the newly elected MPs was called in Dacca, Bhutto warned the members of his own party as well as the other parties in West Pakistan that he would "break their feet" if they attended the session.

The Pakistan government, instead of resolving the matter on the table as was advised by the GOC IV Division, Dacca, and the governor of East Pakistan, opted for a ruthless military operation under the command of General Tikka Khan. As a result, a large number of Bengali Muslims were massacred. "It was utterly pointless," Father would tell us whenever he recounted the events of the bloodiest period of our history.

That, naturally, further deepened the Bengali population's hatred of the people of West Pakistan, particularly the Punjab Army and the Urdu-speaking people of East Pakistan. These Urdu-speaking people had migrated to the east wing from various parts of India, like Calcutta, Bihar, Orissa, UP, CP, and Bombay. They included a good number of government servants and businessmen who had willingly opted for Pakistan at the time of partition.

Unfortunately, there was not much that these Urdu-speaking people could do except watch with tearful eyes the bloody massacre of their Bengali brethren; of course, they didn't want to be a party to the breakup of the country in any way. Many of them, however, indirectly supported the Pakistan Army fighting in the east wing because they believed that their ancestors had rendered sacrifices of men and material for the cause of Pakistan.

With the needless army operation at full blast, Sheikh Mujibur Rehman, who still enjoyed popular support, threatened to secede from Pakistan and unilaterally declare independence of the east wing on March 7, 1971. Before he could do that, he was arrested and kept in a jail in West Pakistan.

Although the situation in East Pakistan appeared calm for some time, the havoc created by General Tikka Khan, which resulted in the deaths of scores of Bengali Muslims, and the subsequent arrest of Sheikh Mujibur Rehman had already dealt a serious blow to the unity of the country.

Migration, Relocation, Joy, Disaster

In view of the fast-changing situation, in May 1971, *daadi*, along with her three grandsons, Syed Ashraf Jamil (a student of the Sylhet Medical College), Syed Khalid Jamil, and Syed Tariq Jamil (who were to appear in the matriculation exam of the Dacca Board) flew to Karachi via Sri Lanka. The three brothers reunited with their father in Rawalpindi, while *daadi* stayed back in Karachi at the residence of Muhammad Nezamul Haque, Father's cousin, to attend the wedding of Uncle Nezam's daughter.

With war clouds still hovering, the wedding was limited, without the usual pomp and ceremony. Ironically, the joy it had brought the two integrating families was soon ruined by the dropping of an Indian bomb on the house of Uncle Nezam. It instantly killed *daadi* and all the children of Uncle Nezam except Shahina, who miraculously remained unhurt.

Fall of Dacca and the Great Massacre: Alas, the East Wing!

After a brief respite, tension rose higher than ever as India openly sided with the Bengalis for its own ulterior motives. The Indians infiltrated their auxiliary as border police forces—the "Mukti Bahinis"—in East Pakistan. Soon the Indian military forces crossed over East Pakistan. It was a declaration of war by India. As feared, it sparked skirmishes between the Pakistan Army and the Indian Army on various fronts. The skirmishes soon escalated and assumed the form of a full-fledged conflict that spread to West Pakistan. The Urdu-speaking people in East Pakistan supported the Pakistan Army till the very last. Religious parties, as well as some political parties in East Pakistan, did not cooperate with the Awami League or the general public; instead, they tried to defend the country by whatever means they had at their disposal. Unfortunately, there was no reinforcement of the Pakistan Army in the east wing, nor any air cover. Consequently, the Pakistan Army under General Niazi laid down their arms in Dacca on December 16, 1971, which resulted in the creation of a new country: Bangladesh.

STJ, like his elder brothers, was an eyewitness to the dismal events that eventually led to the fall of Dhaka and dismemberment of Pakistan in 1971. He recounts the tale of betrayal:

> The people of East Pakistan were politically more conscious than those of West Pakistan. The former were very much attached to the country's political system, so it was not possible to blackmail them in any way. For example, they were very current on political issues, always took keen interest in political activities,

and kept their knowledge up to date through regular reading of newspapers. At that time, there were four major parties in the arena: Awami League, Jamaat-i-Islami, National Awami Party (NAP) of Bhashani, and Muslim League.

The NAP was gifted with great street power. Bhashani, its leader, was so influential that no government could afford to anger him or get away with a policy opposed by him and his followers. Bhashani moved against such policies so swiftly and so strongly that the party in power would either review its policies or totally abolish them.

The Awami League, on the other hand, became more popular after the release of Sheikh Mujibur Rehman. He was a great orator, and his animated speeches attracted people from far and near.

However, Tikka Khan's military operation was the worst move by the West Pakistan rulers: not only did it weaken the chances of a political solution to the crisis, but it also hastened the fall of the east wing; in fact, it proved to be the last nail in the coffin of East Pakistan, a point of no return.

In retrospect, the East Pakistanis had their own reasons for harboring hatred against the west wing. Without doubt, the west wing rulers had deliberately kept them away from vital institutions, like the federal government, the civil service, the armed forces, the police, and the revenue department. They were also deprived of their due share in the development programs of the federal government. In fact, the west wing rulers had made sure that only they controlled all the important positions in the government and the economy; most of these positions were occupied by Pakistanis from the Punjab province. Furthermore, the west wing turned a blind eye to the huge losses suffered by the east wing due to frequent floods and cyclones. There was no plan whatsoever for poverty alleviation. All this had eventually led to a strong feeling of deprivation among the people of the east wing.

Mujibur Rehman was fully aware of the anti-east policies of the west wing and cited them profusely whenever and wherever he got the opportunity. In his fiery public speeches, he would urge his followers to unite against what he called the hostile posture of the west wing. His arguments made a lot of sense and appealed to the people. Therefore, in no time, the whole political climate underwent a sea change, and in the general elections that followed, the Awami League, as was projected, won a majority, losing only two seats in all of East Pakistan. The message was loud and clear: Mujib had won the right to form the government.

However, the west wing politicians refused to accept the verdict of the people. There was no justification for their refusal. Guided by their lust for control, they wanted to snatch power by hook or by crook. The seeds of discord were thus sown, and a wide gulf of mistrust was created between the two wings.

The eventual dismemberment of Pakistan was extremely tragic, not only for the Muslims of Pakistan and South Asia but also for the entire Muslim world. The aftermath was ruthless and bloody. The Indian Army, abetted by the so-called nationalist Bengalis, massacred thousands of Urdu-speaking people and a fairly large number of religious-minded Bengali Muslims. It was deliberate and systematic. In addition, properties of Urdu-speaking Muslims in East Pakistan were looted and their homes forcibly occupied by the local people and "revolutionary" Bengalis.

To save their lives, many Urdu-speaking Muslims fled to West Pakistan through Nepal. The government of Nepal was kind enough to allow their entry. It fully sympathized with the migrants and helped them repatriate to Pakistan. The Pakistan embassy in Nepal also played a commendable role in that hour of need.

Unfortunately, a good number of Urdu-speaking Muslims who wanted to migrate to West Pakistan could not do so because they didn't have the resources to travel. Even today, many of them are languishing in various Red Cross camps in Dhaka and other places. Their total number is about two hundred and fifty thousand. They are Pakistanis by all cannons of law. The Bangladesh government is apparently not interested in improving their condition, and the Pakistan government is unwilling to repatriate and settle them in Pakistan. It's a heartless situation! The result is these Pakistanis are rotting in camps without any means of livelihood, without proper nutrition, clothing, or education. It is ironic that those who had fought and voted for Pakistan are not welcome in their own homeland! There is every reason to fear that these stranded Pakistanis will eventually be forced to leave Bangladesh and seek refuge elsewhere, most probably in India. That would be most unfortunate.

SKJ, who was also an eyewitness to the gloomy episode of 1971, remembers the event as follows:

It was a terrible night when the West Pakistan Army launched the operation in March 1971. The whole sky was lit up as a result of endless firing and dropping of bombs. It was a day of unspeakable horror. Oblivious to what was going on around us, we ascended to the roof of our house to witness the events. It was another *tandaily* (foolish undertaking) on our part. The morning after, every Bengali vacated the Magh Bazaar area where we lived, except one who was our next-door neighbor. I don't remember his name, but he was a loner. The night after the operation we heard him yell, *"ek abray patla koredeshi!"* ('I'm passing loose stools out of fear!')

The escape from Magh Bazaar to Muhammadpur wasn't easy. The four of us, SAJ, STJ, *daadi*, and I, began our long journey with nothing but faith in Allah as the only guiding principle and escort. The distance from Magh Bazaar to Muhammadpur was about seven kilometers, if one took the shortcut across the railway track. Believe it or not, *daadi*, who was seventy then, along with the three of us covered the entire distance on foot. Fortunately, we didn't face any untoward situation on the way. We were also lucky because by that time, the West Pakistan Army had taken full control of the city. Those who could not flee or were too slow to escape were attacked, hurt, or killed by Mukti Bahini rebels.

Before fleeing, we had hurriedly sold as many household items as we could to the first buyers at throwaway prices. These included a few charpoys, used pipes, and pieces of wood and timber that Father had made us save for a rainy day. Cutting a long story short, *sub kutch chopat ho gia!* (All was ruined!).

Years later we learned that the money from the premigration sale was not saved by the brothers; it was instead spent on buying *rasgullas,* the incredibly yummy sweet balls! The only thing the brothers couldn't sell was the record player Father had brought from Japan. This flat, gray record player continued to entertain us for a number of years after we migrated to Rawalpindi in May 1971.

Also, during his service in East Pakistan, Father had acquired some immovable properties, including a 280-square-yard plot in Naya Tola, Magh Bazaar, on which he had built a three-bedroom house, and a 600-square-yard plot in Muhammadpur Housing Estate, on which he had constructed a house with an attached servants' quarters. It was rented out to a businessman from Punjab.

Migration to West Pakistan, however, deprived Father of the above properties. His repeated pleas for compensation fell on deaf ears. The concerned authorities in West Pakistan were of no help whatsoever. Father, however, always kept the land ownership documents and files in safe custody, hoping that someday some God-fearing officer would reactivate the dormant files and help settle a long standing issue. That day hasn't dawned yet.

Ashfaq Bhai's Tale of Survival

"There's no doubt that I am a Bihari. And I am proud of being a Bihari. I belong to that soil. I was born in Bihar, you know."

Ashfaq bhai, affectionately called Ashfaqi by some of us, was seated in his jam-packed tire shop at Melody Market, Islamabad, when I stepped in.

"Salaam, Sabir," he said and gestured me to sit down. There were no customers in the shop. I placed myself on a small wooden bench, the most out-of-place object in the highly rubberized setting.

"Unlike most of my Bihari relatives and friends, who would never reveal their identity for fear of being singled out or discriminated against, I never shy away from telling people that I am a Bihari, that I belong to as eminent a place as Bihar. I'm not a coward."

Ashfaq bhai's conviction impressed me. "But there's a great misconception about Biharis," I said.

"You are right," he said. "The general impression isn't good. But that's not correct. Some people wrongly assume that Biharis are a poor people, that they would easily resort to begging for a living. That is utter nonsense, I can tell you. The begging men and women you see around mosques, marketplaces, or other public sites are not Biharis. They are ordinary locals who use the 'Bihari card,' as it were, to gain the sympathies of the passersby. I can tell you without a shred of doubt that a true Bihari would die rather than beg for money."

"What happened to the thousands of Biharis stranded in Bangladesh?" I inquired.

"It's a pity that no one talks about them anymore. Only 2 percent of Biharis could migrate to Pakistan at the time of fall of Dhaka. Over two hundred thousand of them are still languishing in squalid camps in Bangladesh. It's a miserable life for them. Go and see for yourself. They are still counting on Pakistan for repatriation, despite years of heartless indifference on our part. But, I think, a ray of hope still kindles in their wounded hearts."

"True," I said, endorsing his point that Biharis had played a pivotal role in the creation of Pakistan. Knowing that Ashfaq bhai was a witness to the bloody riots of 1971, I posed the inevitable question.

"I was a trainee salesman at the Kohinoor Chemical Company," he told me, "where my father had served for years. Those were unpredictable times. The heartrending news was that Dacca had fallen to the enemy and that the Pakistan Army had surrendered to the tearful shock of the whole nation. But I was not dismayed."

"Where were you at that time?" I asked.

"When the news of the Fall reached me, I was at work. Moeenuddin, our company's head, was a refined Bengali with a rare clarity of vision. When the riots broke out, he was in Chittagong on a three-month official visit. I had a fair idea of the kind of suffering his family was going through in his absence. I began to feel a strong moral pressure to inquire about them and do whatever I could to help them in their hour of need. They were stationed in Dacca, the epicenter of the bloody conflict and chaos. In fact, the place where Moeen's family lived was one of the besieged areas. But I decided to take the risk. All the way to the bus stop, I came across mutilated bodies of men, women, and children slain without mercy. It was a ghastly spectacle. I quickened my pace to get to the bus stop, only to find that the last bus had left the station. I was frustrated, but I didn't lose hope. I set off on foot. It was a dangerous thing to do; the chances of getting killed by a stray bullet were very high. But, thank God, I safely reached Moeenuddin's house.

"Mrs. Moeenuddin urged me to prolong my stay in Dacca for security reasons. She had three little daughters to guard, and there was no male family member at home. My sense of duty was alive, and I agreed to delay my return.

"Two times a week I visited them with a bagful of food supplies. I was happy that now there was no need for them to venture out of their house. Fortunately, the children's uncle, who resided in a relatively peaceful district, soon came to their rescue, which made them feel more secure. My job was over for the time being, and I returned home."

"Can you recall some of the worst fears of those days?" I interrupted.

"We lived in Chowk Bazaar, which was once a busy shopping center, but when things started to get worse, it was quickly paralyzed. The drama of betrayal and bloody politics, now in its advanced stage, was affecting every aspect of life. A huge sense of insecurity and uncertainty had crippled all human activity. A day after the Fall, I still remember, someone knocked at our door. First, it was gentle, then a loud bang that sent shivers down my spine. It was scary. My mother huddled me up. I could hear my heart pound with tremendous force. I frantically moved my eyes in all directions to look for an exit. There was none.

"'Open the door,' barked the men shaking the door. I stared inquiringly at my mother and my sister. They were both silent as stone. Without a second thought, I rushed to unlock the door. I had no other option; the mobsters were hell-bent on destroying the door.

"Four dismally dressed rascals broke in. They all had dense moustaches. Two of them had pistols in their hands, while the other two carried iron rods. My mother clutched my little sister to her shaking body.

"'Take out all the money you have,' shouted one of them.

"'Wolves!' I cursed them without moving my lips. My mother begged them not to shoot. She tossed them the key to the only cabinet in the house. They searched for money but found only a little, for that was all we had. Frustrated, they grabbed a transistor and a pair of tattered shoes. The ordeal was not over yet.

"'You, you're to come with us. And you, and you.' One of them, the one who appeared to be the ring leader, pointed toward Ishtiaq, my younger brother; his friend Saleem, who had come all the way to meet him; and me.

"My mother pleaded, in vain, for mercy. They dragged the three of us away to an unknown destination.

"It was a cold December afternoon. There was a despicable chill in the air. We brothers had very little clothing on; our bones ached all over. About midway, one of them, the one holding the pistol, commanded us to stop. We obeyed without a second thought. Another tied our hands and blindfolded us. Then all of us resumed the journey. It was a long and strenuous journey. We didn't have any idea about time or place.

"They all remained silent until we reached a place they called *adda* (station). A silly question-answer session followed, of which I could not make any head or tail. Ishtiaq had once been with the East Pakistan Civil Armed Forces, the fact of which might have led to our arrests. But I was not sure Ishtiaq's army connection had anything to do with our kidnapping.

"On a half-broken, stumbling boat, we crossed a river and got to the other side. For the first time, I sensed that something was terribly wrong. I could smell danger like one smells garlic.

"Then I heard one of them quietly loading his pistol. Ishtiaq's hand brushed mine, for he too had smelt the danger.

"Next, I felt a current of warm breath stroke my face; it smelt of onion. Then, I felt something cold and metallic, a pistol most probably, against the flesh of my neck. It sent shivers down my back and made me sweat again. Was it the end of the road for us? Was it the end of everything? Repent! Seek God's forgiveness! Recite the Kalma! That was all I could think of.

"Quite tormenting it was to lose all hope so quickly!

"But then the impossible happened. Someone came running toward us shouting, 'Daro, Daro!' It was a familiar voice. I felt a sudden release of pressure on my neck.

"'Hold it, hold it! Don't shoot!' the running man was yelling. He gestured the gang leader, Mangi, not to shoot us. "You have the wrong men," he spoke breathlessly.

"It was Hafeez Kalu, my Bengali friend, an angel sent by God. He had joined Mukti Bahinis, the resistance movement, but was still my friend.

"Kalu talked the gang leader into letting us go; of course, we had nothing to do with their miseries. Mangi and his men returned to me the little money they had looted.

"I returned to work after a week or so. Moeenuddin embraced me. I told him how Ishtiaq and I had run away from the clutches of death. He burst into tears. To thank me for the little work I had done to help his family, he promoted me to manage the bills of the company."

"How did you manage to migrate to West Pakistan?" I asked.

"Colonel Aslam was my father's friend. His son, Mehmud, was martyred in the struggle. A gem of great value was he; he died for an idea. One day Colonel Aslam summoned me and urged me to migrate to West Pakistan as early as possible, for the situation in East Pakistan was getting worse by the day. To my utter amazement, he gave me his dead son's passport! He insisted that I take it. I took it with tears rolling down my cheeks.

"Two years after the bloody conflict, one hazy morning, I landed at Karachi airport. It was a new place, and I had a new name. It was a strange feeling!"

 # Magh Bazaar (Moghbazar)

IT IS IMPOSSIBLE FOR ME TO recall the ins and outs of Magh Bazaar, for I was only three or four when our family left their ancestral hometown for a safer district in West Pakistan. Nevertheless, the name Magh Bazaar has always been with us, more on the lips of our parents and elder brothers than on those of the younger members of the family. Therefore, virtually all that I know today about this small Dhaka town, all that I share with you here, is based on tales told by elder brothers, chiefly STJ and SKJ.

Also known as Naya Tola, Magh Bazaar was famous for the tomb of Shah Sahib, a notable saint who had graced the land in the distant past and whose disciples and devotees were great in number. The tomb, better known as Shah Sahib ki Bari (House of Shah Sahib), was built in the early sixties on the banks of River Tongi.

The town was mostly inhabited by upright Bengali Muslims, who lived in huts made of bamboo wood and mud and tin roofs. Some educated Urdu-speaking Muslims purchased land there and constructed their brick houses. Their arrival and settlement in Magh Bazaar paved the way for education and prosperity in the area.

The natives welcomed their Urdu-speaking brothers and sisters and extended all possible support. In fact, a committee comprising Urdu- and Bengali-speaking residents was formed to manage the local affairs, which included road construction, sewage, and the holding of a weekly bazaar. Father, who enjoyed great respect in the area for being an upright gentleman, firm in commitment, was chosen to head the committee. Another reason for his selection was his excellent knowledge of Islamic teachings;

thus, upon request, he would deliver sermons in local *Milaad* congregations. He was also entrusted with slaughtering hens, goats, and cows in the Islamic manner.

Father's Activities in Magh Bazaar; His Wisdom and Foresight; Mushtaq, the "Nutcase"

Father had lost his father at the age of two. This, however, had not demoralized him, as he went on to achieve remarkable success as a well-educated and disciplined member of the family.

Never did Father show any sign of weakness; in fact, he always turned his weakness into strength, embraced all kinds of challenges, and faced threats very boldly. A truly self-made man was he.

We, for instance, never saw Father intimidated or panic-stricken in any kind of situation. Instead, he used his distinctive thinking ability to outsmart his opponents or turn them into comrades.

STJ vividly recalls Father's use of his management skills on more than one occasion.

Magh Bazaar, where we lived, was predominantly occupied by natives co-existing with a minority of Urdu-speaking families; no problems between the two groups ever cropped up because Father worked hard to maintain a good relationship with almost everybody around. They all lived happily as one integrated family.

Secondly, through strict adherence to the norms of good behavior, Father had earned the reputation of being a man of integrity. The entire local population had full faith in him, and no wrong could ever be associated with him.

Then, one scorching summer, something happened that tested Father's patience and stretched it to its limit.

It all began when a fairly rich but arrogant family moved into the area. The family head, an undersized man in his fifties, was an officer in the Police Department. Most of the locals did not like him, for they had found him excessively proud and, therefore, unfit for any kind of social relationship or association.

This man had two sons. The elder, Mushtaq, was a "nutcase" and was despised by the natives for maligning the Bangla-speaking residents and pitting them against the Urdu-speaking people of the area. In fact, he would go to the extent of calling the Urdu-speaking boys names and habitually teasing school-going girls in the neighborhood.

Mushtaq was doing all this, the neighbors believed, on account of his father's powerful job in the police department, something he drew all his strength and confidence from. Gradually, to everyone's dismay, he became a nuisance.

We were strictly advised by Father not to get offended, but adopt a policy of indifference, as any reaction could aggravate the situation. Indifference, however, had no impact on Mushtaq: he continued to fool around, appearing outside our house several times a day and routinely hurling abuses at us and our neighbors.

One person who was most disturbed by Mushtaq's stupid antics was SAJ. Because Father had strictly told us to ignore Mushtaq, there was not much we could do except remain silent. That was what SAJ did, though he knew that it was adversely affecting his studies.

But there is a limit to what a man can tolerate! Mushtaq's irritating presence annoyed SAJ so much that one day SAJ quit his studies all of a sudden and scurried out of his room at the speed of light. He grabbed Mushtaq by his shoulder, lifted him up, slammed him onto the ground, sat over his chest, and launched a massive attack with his fists on Mushtaq's face, wounding him seriously.

This was too much for Mushtaq. The bloody treatment had jolted him and apparently taught him a useful lesson. He fled the scene like a coward and was not spotted in the area for many days thereafter.

It was the holy month of Ramadan when Mushtaq reappeared, this time with a lot more venom in his eyes and a couple of fleshy bodyguards at his side. It wasn't a very impressive sight. Obviously, Mushtaq hadn't learned his lesson. When Father was informed of his return, to our surprise he urged us to follow the old policy of indifference.

However, elsewhere in the vicinity, something spicier was cooking in the minds of a group of young Bengali- and Urdu-speaking buddies, headed by Mansoor, Uncle Bashir's son. After holding several street-corner meetings, the group came to the conclusion that SAJ's treatment of Mushtaq had not done enough to bring the cop's son to his senses; therefore, it was necessary to look for some stronger dose for Mushtaq.

After further deliberations, the group finalized a scheme: they would leave the mosque in the middle of the Taraveeh prayers without anyone noticing and assemble at a specified street corner. Then they would go on to beat up Mushtaq and his allies and, without wasting time, return to the mosque to rejoin the prayers.

There was nothing holy about the scheme. The result was bloody: Mushtaq and his men received multiple injuries to their heads and faces, but nothing alarming. As expected, it infuriated Mushtaq's father, who galloped out of his quarters with a bunch of his supporters and began shouting and yelling outside our house. It was pretty dark already, and the male members of the family were still in the mosque performing their Taraveeh prayers. The ladies of the house and those of some other houses in the area, unsettled by the sudden commotion, stepped out with wide eyes and frightened faces to find out what was happening.

Not caring in the least about the norms and traditions, Mushtaq's father yelled at the ladies and said things that were offensive and rude and threatening, which forced the ladies to lock themselves up in their respective houses.

As soon as the men returned from the mosque, the ladies reported every little detail of what had happened in the men's absence. It angered Uncle Bashir the most, so much that he raced out of his room like a raging thunderstorm, vowing to hack Mushtaq's father to death. But Father seized his hand and pulled him inside.

The next day, taking advantage of his service in the police department, Mushtaq's father lodged a complaint at the local police station and named Father, Uncle Bashir, Mansoor, and a few others in the first information report. Since the incident involved many local families, the police invited a few elders of the community to meet in the Azad Club; the idea was to resolve the matter in a peaceful way.

The complainant, Mushtaq, was asked to narrate the incident. Most of the things he said about Mansoor and his friends beating him up were true; however, in an attempt to make his case stronger, he made the awful mistake of accusing Father of a crime he hadn't committed. In his statement, Mushtaq claimed that he had seen Father holding a rifle and threatening to kill him.

Upon hearing this, Mansoor and his friends, who

knew that it was not true, stood up and interrupted Mushtaq. Father motioned for them to sit down and keep quiet until Mushtaq was done with his statement.

Mushtaq's blunder, his lie about Father, actually turned the case against him. Father was confident that there would be many in the area willing to appear as witnesses to confirm that he had been performing his Taraveeh prayers in the mosque at the time of the incident.

That is exactly what happened. Many residents turned up to testify against Mushtaq. As a result, the police declared Mushtaq's statement a fabrication, a mere concoction, and closed the case.

It was Father's wisdom and foresight that had saved Mansoor and others that day, as any further probe into the matter would surely have uncovered the bloody beating of Mushtaq. Had that happened, Mansoor and his men would have found themselves in the lockup.

Father the Hunter? Yes!

Father was very fond of hunting halal birds whenever and wherever an opportunity came his way with his neatly kept single-bore rifle.

On the day set aside for hunting, at least once a month, Father would dress up in shirt and trousers, put on a felt hat, and carry the rifle slung around his right shoulder, the bullets firmly stacked in his trouser pocket.

Most of the hunters in Father's group were his close friends, chiefly Uncle Ziauddin. Together, during the many expeditions, they would stride away from the town center to where the birds descended in groups of twos and threes or more in search of food. The areas they frequently visited included Nama, Tejgaon, Gulshan (now a posh area of Dhaka), and the adjoining villages.

Sometimes a bunch of family kids also accompanied the hunters. Their real aim would be to collect the empty shells and the fallen birds, and to make arrangements for the slaughtering of the birds in the Islamic manner.

Although hunting served as a great adventure and a kind of emotional release, it sometimes led to incredible situations. Once, for example, Father spotted a pair of king storks. He aimed at one of them and fired. The bullet hit the bird and it collapsed, while the other stayed amazingly still as if nothing had happened. Seeing this, Father motioned the picker boys to wait, then he took aim at the other bird, the one unaffected by the death of his partner, and fired. The bullet pierced his left leg, and he too collapsed!

When Father returned home and narrated the bizarre incident to his family and friends, nobody believed him. It sounded extremely strange to them that one of the two birds had remained unaffected by the demise of his close-standing partner, even though the firing sound was thunderous enough to wake up the whole community. A number of questions were asked to solve the mystery. "Was the other bird deaf? Was he too lost in a dreamy world of his own? Did his partner's sudden death force him to commit suicide?"

Whatever the reason, during the course of these trips, the hunters were able to compile their own little hunting dictionary; they invented words and some unique terms that eventually became part of their everyday conversation. For example, "unjik" was used for a misfire; "alfaqaloo" meant hitting the target; and "alshoosha" referred to missing a target that did not move at all.

The target birds mostly included king storks (*bugla*), doves, and pigeons. Thanks to Father's perfect vision and quick reflexes, plus his overwhelming interest in hunting, the targets rarely got away.

The hunted birds were cooked at home, and part of the meat was distributed among close family friends, like Uncle Bashir and

Uncle Ziauddin. Everybody would thoroughly enjoy the feast and the humor and the gossip associated with it.

Cooking the hunted bird, however, meant a lot of additional work for Mother. Though she didn't hate to do it, she didn't like it either. Once, for example, she was extremely enraged when Father brought home a forest rabbit. Mother agreed to cook the herbivore only reluctantly, as she was convinced nobody would ever taste the "cat-like" meat. "I remember," recalls STJ, "we did try it, unwillingly of course, just for the sake of tasting it, but it was hard to enjoy the meat. The very sight of it was sickening. Above all, we had never eaten a rabbit before, though it was very much halal."

Father's single-bore rifle was part of our luggage when we migrated from Dacca to Rawalpindi in 1971. But it was never used by Father or anybody else in the family again. It was probably sold or donated to someone just before we left Rawalpindi to settle permanently in Islamabad.

Father's Talent for Trade?

A remarkable event in the life of Father was his very bold initiative of opening a grocery store in Magh Bazaar, in partnership with Uncle Ziauddin, his close friend. The idea was to generate some additional income to meet the needs of the two growing families. Unfortunately, it did not work out well due to inexperience and inattention, for both the partners were extremely busy in their government jobs and household duties.

But perhaps the foremost reason for the failure of the business was that neither of the partners was business-minded. They were hoping to run the store on the model of cooperatives, where the objective is not to make profit, but to provide a platform for people to buy groceries at affordable prices.

Interestingly, some customers of the store believed that the undoing of the venture was largely due to the hiring of a shopkeeper with defective eyes. He took too much time counting the coins and notes and had great difficulty reading the price tags for the customers. Worst of all, some would pretend to be customers (mostly teenagers) and take advantage of his poor eyesight, stealing stuff from the shop almost every day and getting away with it.

Surprisingly, among those who shoplifted things every now and then included SAJ, SKJ, STJ, and Uncle Bashir's sons, to name only a few. For sure, they all did it for fun, to enjoy free toffees and biscuits and stuff like that. This explains why the venture failed miserably, and the two partners were forced to close it down. The unsold goods were then equally divided between the partners.

Father's Helping Attitude toward Kith and Kin

Father, by nature, had always been very helpful to people within as well as outside the family. Whenever people approached him for advice or assistance, he would lend them a hand without expecting a reward in return. There are many examples of Father's obliging disposition.

For instance, he always welcomed our cousins Arif bhai, Asif bhai, and Iqbal bhai, who stayed in our house for as many days as they wished and thoroughly enjoyed Father's company and hospitality. They visited us from other cities and towns in connection with job interviews or education or mere excursion.

He also welcomed our maternal uncle and his family and our paternal uncles and their families to stay at our place in Rawalpindi soon after their migration from Dacca and other parts of East Pakistan. Father willingly let them stay at our place until they were in a position to move to their own houses.

Father also embraced Uncle Nasim and let him stay at our home when the latter was asked to vacate his own brother's house because of "a problem."

Father also took good care of his widowed sister and her

daughters in India by extending his full cooperation, moral as well as monetary, in the matter of the daughters' marriages.

All this Father was able to achieve by limiting the comforts of his own children, though he was never unmindful of their rights. Of course we fully understood Father's noble intentions and never complained; it never occurred to us that we were being deprived of any privileges. Father didn't just believe in the rights of children, relatives, and neighbors enshrined in the Islamic teachings, but he also practiced the teachings in his life.

Father's Commendable Role during the 1970–71 Crisis

STJ recalls Father's significant role during the 1970–71 crisis as follows.

> Being very active in the small town of Naya Tola, Father always did things to keep the local people together. For example, during the East Pakistan crisis, Father was quick to set up a peace committee comprised of elders from the area with its sole purpose being to protect the locals and prevent any outsiders from destroying the peace of the neighborhood.
>
> Father's initiative did wonders: the peace committee was able to curb the few awkward situations that had surfaced during the worst days of the crisis. These situations involved a handful of local men who were deeply prejudiced against the minority Urdu-speaking residents and would never miss an opportunity to malign them. It was Father's timely intervention that had prevented such unfortunate situations from getting out of control.
>
> Father would have continued to play his reconciliatory role in Naya Tola had he not been selected for posting in the Ministry of Defence, Rawalpindi. Convinced

that the Almighty had other plans for him, Father accepted the offer, and, in January 1971, moved to Rawalpindi. Mother and eight of the children joined him a month later; the remaining three, STJ, SKJ, and SAJ, along with grandmother, joined the rest of the family in May the same year. SAJ, who was studying medicine at Sylhet Medical College, Sylhet, at the time of the crisis, had an awful time leaving the area unharmed and later described his escape as "scary and narrow."

The Magh Bazaar House and Its Surroundings

"Our house in Magh Bazaar," recalls SKJ, "was a *pukka* building made of cement, iron, and bricks. It had a large room, a small room, and a verandah. As the size of our family increased, one more living room, a bathroom, and a separate kitchen facing the verandah were added. There were two or three *chowkis* (wooden bed frames) in the bigger room, and there was also a dining table that was used as bed at night by SAJ. Since the surrounding area was a breeding ground for mosquitoes and similar insects, mosquito nets were almost always used at night. There was a big open space in front of the house, where grandmother used to grow some vegetables. We also had goats, chickens, and ducks of our own. Living in the Magh Bazaar House was a lot of fun."

Magh Bazaar had more than its share of ponds and lakes where local lads practiced and demonstrated their swimming skills in the scorching heat of the summer. The shows were so captivating that even a shy fellow like STJ was inspired and motivated to learn the art. It took him just a few dives to master it, and he followed it up with daring dips every now and then, skipping school for the purpose.

Magh Bazaar was once the stage of a fascinating incident that took place in one of the most eventful years in the lives of SAJ, SKJ, and STJ. SAJ was its key character, while SKJ and STJ played supporting roles. It was one of the brothers' fruit-stealing ventures; the venue was the neighbor's orchard.

STJ recalls the event: "As we were busy plucking and eating one fruit after another and stuffing as many as we could into our pockets—something we enjoyed doing on a regular basis—the owner of the orchard, a dangerous-looking fellow of a mean variety, spotted us. He shouted abuses at us and chased us at the speed of light. In a matter of seconds, what began as a fun activity turned into a life-saving exercise."

While SKJ and STJ were able to outrun the breathless neighbor, SAJ was not so lucky. He stumbled and fell down, and before he could get up, the robust neighbor's iron hands were firmly planted on SAJ's shoulders. The neighbor, probably a Bengali (no offense against Bengalis), was naturally furious; his reddening face and bulging eyes had turned him into a monster. "His stare was penetrating enough to frighten off grown-ups, let alone kids," SAJ remembers.

Although SAJ was greatly frustrated at not being able to smell this danger in advance, he didn't give up. He waited patiently for the neighbor to loosen his grip. When the hefty guy twisted his right hand just a bit to scratch his back, SAJ wriggled out of the painful lock and ran to safety. It was indeed a lucky escape, one that led the brothers to refrain from any further ventures.

Lions Model School

This was probably the first Urdu medium school set up in Magh Bazaar by a group of Urdu-speaking Muslims from India who mostly came from the Bihar province. Father, who at that time was working in the East Pakistan Civil Service as its only graduate in town, headed the group. He enjoyed the moral support of many neighbors, including Ali Akbar and Bashir Chacha.

To the utter amazement of the inhabitants, the legendary Lions Club had donated ten thousand rupees to establish the school on the condition that it be named Lions Model School.

Some members of the group were outraged by this bizarre precondition, but Father, who was well aware of the pressing need for such a school in the area, talked the angry members into accepting the club's demand, for it promised greater good to the whole community.

Once the name issue was resolved, the foundation of the school was laid by Mr. Isfahani, the president of the club. Mr. Isfahani and his family had migrated from Iran and settled in Piyara Bagh, some three miles from downtown Magh Bazaar. In fact, all the migrant Iranian families had settled in what later came to be known as the Isfahani Colony. They mostly communicated in Persian but also understood and spoke Urdu.

The colony was protected by a fortified wall and was guarded round the clock by paid security personnel. It had just one entrance-exit gate. A grove of towering trees almost completely hid the colony from the outside world and mystified the whole area. In fact, the colony gave the impression of being a tiny city provided with all the amenities of life, in stark contrast with the adjoining areas. The Isfahanis had, for instance, their own school, their own cricket team, and their own shopping center.

The Lions Model School organized sport events every year, first inside the Isfahani Colony and later on a public field. They were all sponsored by the Lions Club, and Mr. Isfahani would grace the events as chief guest. Being the head of the management committee, Father always enjoyed the privilege of sitting next to Mr. Isfahani.

Most probably because of his close association with Mr. Isfahani, Father was obliged to send SAJ, SKJ, and STJ to the Lions Model School for their elementary education. Six-year-old SKJ and four-year-old STJ were enrolled in the same class, whereas SAJ, being older, was placed three or four classes ahead of them. For a year or so the three brothers went to the same school. Then SAJ was shifted to Government High School (GHS), Moti Jheel, because the Lions didn't offer any schooling beyond the elementary. Located in downtown Dacca, GHS ranked as a first-class learning center catering to the needs of a growing population.

Although the brothers' first few school years were devoid of any record-breaking achievements, they were by no means academically bleak, with the possible exception of SKJ, who had quickly earned the reputation of being less gifted than the other two. For example, in the elementary school, SKJ had become known as a casual happy-go-lucky wanderer who thought it funny to take studies seriously. He concentrated more on sports like sack-jumping, egg-in-spoon relay, and relay racing. No wonder he was able to grab the second prize in the unusual event of sack-racing. Moreover, by virtue of his sheer physical strength, SKJ always dominated the boys of his age group. A fighter by nature, he would seldom spare anyone, not even his skinny younger brother STJ.

SKJ depended a great deal on STJ for academic assistance. This assistance was generously provided by STJ not only at home and school but also in the dreaded examination halls, where SKJ would purposely sit next to him or right behind him, always on the edge of his seat. This would enable him to peek at STJ's answer sheet "whenever the invigilator wasn't looking." Also, at SKJ's insistence, STJ would sometimes slow down his writing speed to let SKJ catch up with him. This dangerous operation luckily didn't lead to their arrest or punishment or expulsion from school.

When SKJ and STJ passed Class 4, they too were transferred to GHS, Moti Jheel, where SAJ, enrolled in Class 8, was already showing great signs of progress. The reunion of the brothers brought them immense joy, as they always derived strength from one another. Above all, it saved Father some money in tuition fees.

Cricket and Other Attractions

Magh Bazaar was replete with attractions: kite flying, lutto, marbles, swimming, cricket, card games, badminton, *dareecha*, steel ring, tire pushing, *satt chaara*, and bombastic, to name a few. The most popular of these were cricket and kite flying.

The Lions Club Cricket Team (LCCT), of which SKJ and STJ were active members, was the brainchild of young enthusiasts who had done hard work to collect donations from the locals to buy cricket equipment and clothing. The next important step for the boys was to pick a ground and prepare a pitch. After careful thought, the ground on the banks of the Nama River was chosen, and a pitch was marked on it right away. As soon as it was ready, the young boys who had toiled day and night to make it a reality began their long practice sessions. In no time, these boys were ready to challenge their more experienced counterparts representing the other cricket teams of the region.

The matches that followed boosted the confidence of the LCCT players. They took on one team after another and routed most of them. It wasn't just confidence that was doing the trick—it was also the hostile pace attack of Nurul and the baffling spin of Karaar. The team's batting strength, represented by openers little Mansoor and hefty SKJ, was also instrumental in crushing the opponents. SKJ in particular, having more might than mind, was a very hard hitter of the cricket ball.

But in a little while, things started to go wrong. It all began when Tejgaon BG Press cricket team, which for sure included no babies, was needlessly provoked and challenged. The LCCT were not smart enough to refuse to take them on. A series of wins against the weaker teams had filled them with too much pride and given them the false assurance that they could make minced meat of the formidable BG Press.

The LCCT were terribly wrong in their assumptions. The contest proved to be a case of sheer miscalculation and misjudgment. On the day of the great clash, expectations were higher than ever and tension gripped the LCCT players. It became evident in the very first over when little Mansoor of the LCCT missed a rising ball. The ball kissed his tender chin with such force that two of his front teeth instantly flew out of his mouth, leaving a pool of blood behind. Poor Mansoor was groaning with pain when the close-in fielders ran up to him to offer free advice and damage assessment. It was an extremely awkward situation, so the game was called off.

That was not all. The LCCT met a similar fate when they faced the Isfahanis in the next encounter, which took place in the Isfahani Ground. The Isfahani batsmen thrashed the LCCT bowlers all over the place, and one of them even hit seventy-odd runs without getting out. Even the experienced Nurul was not spared; they made forty in his five overs. The frustration and disappointment that followed haunted the LCCT players for weeks and months.

Rolling the *Chakka* for Fun!

Another game that Magh Bazaar boys enjoyed playing was called *chakka* rolling. It simply consisted of running parallel to a *chakka*, a circular steel wire or rod kept rolling with the help of a wooden stick or twig.

For many local kids who belonged to poor families, it was a major—and in some cases, the only—summer pastime. It was not at all expensive, for the *chakka* could easily be made at home using leftover scraps.

According to STJ, "The whole idea was to run alongside the *chakka* without letting it go still. Whoever ran the longest distance without letting it go static won the game."

Although *chakka* rolling was not an Olympic sport, it was without doubt a source of genuine amusement; besides, it enabled the participating kids to learn the art of balancing early on in life. And since it involved a lot of running, it also did a wealth of good for the runners' legs.

Father, however, didn't really like the sport. He never considered it a gentleman's choice. With that in mind, SKJ and STJ rolled the *chakka* only when Father was not around.

Cigarette Empties

Another recreational activity that the Magh Bazaar youth engaged themselves in was the collection of empty cigarette packets. The boys taking part in the activity took turns aiming at the empties with a pebble or stone, and whoever hit a pack first won all the empties. It resembled to a certain extent a card game played with cards of different values. The empties thus collected were kept as treasure at a safe and secure place inside the house.

To many locals, it was more of a fun-packed hobby than a game. To others, it unnecessarily exposed the young minds to "cool brand names" that the boys would eventually memorize, which in turn could possibly motivate them to take up smoking later in life.

Mystery, or Better Call It Nama!

Away from the charms and attractions of Magh Bazaar, adjacent to Naya Tola (Shah Sahib Bari), stood a place that haunted its residents for years on end: Nama.

It was essentially a low-lying area, more like a fertile jungle, a safe haven for snakes, squirrels, rats, lizards, moles, dogs, cats, monkeys, birds, and whatnot. It was a dreadful district, a terrifying terrain, so much so that walking across the place after nightfall was almost out of the question.

Nama had earned this reputation by staging quite a few gruesome events. The most horrific of them were the hanging of Maqsood Gawala, the drowning of Boba, the demonizing of Nurul, and the hanging of a poor native woman.

The Hanging of Maqsood Gawala

The natives of Naya Tola often complained of hearing strange voices and seeing ghostly faces, some as black as charcoal. Once three brothers returning from Nama claimed to have seen at least six headless, naked men occupying a certain bamboo tree. Of course no one believed them, yet people feared to go there after sunset.

In the immediate vicinity of Shah Sahib Bari lived Maqsood Gawala, a stout fellow of dark complexion and bulging eyes. Strangely, he lived in a primitive hut despite being the richest *gawala* (milkman) in town. He was in his early forties and married with no children. Childlessness troubled him once in a blue moon, but Maqsood was not angry with God. As a matter of fact, he was not cross with any creature on earth.

The inhabitants of Shah Sahib Bari were mostly farmers who took their cattle to Nama for grazing. They always moved in groups of two or three for security reasons. Maqsood also ventured out with his cows, but he enjoyed wandering alone.

One quiet September morning, Maqsood woke up earlier than usual, offered his predawn prayers, and sat down to milk his reluctant cows. These cows he had bought recently to meet the natives' growing demand for milk. As he began to milk one of the cows, he noticed that the small piece of rope tied around the cow's neck was worn out in places. It startled Maqsood; he could not make head or tail of it, for he had never seen such a thing before.

Maqsood's wife, Akhtari Begum, who later narrated the day's gloomy events to the neighbors, was a woman known for her nobility and faithfulness. She could read and write, and girls in the neighborhood came to her to learn cooking and stitching. That morning she served her husband with chapattis and *saag*, Maqsood's favorite dish. He ate an extra chapatti that day before paddling out to distribute milk.

But to the great shock of Akhtari Begum and her neighbors, Maqsood didn't return home that day. His wife kept waiting for him until it got depressingly dark. She thought about seeking her neighbors' help, but, being alone, she decided against it. She consoled herself by thinking positive: "His bicycle must have broken down or something else must have come up. His friend Abdul must have forced him to spend the night at his place," which he sometimes did.

None of that had actually happened. In fact, the next morning, residents of Shah Sahib Bari woke up to a gruesome sight: Maqsood Gawala hanging by a banyan tree. It struck terror into the hearts of the natives.

No one had a clue what had happened.

The news of the mysterious death of Maqsood Gawala spread like jungle fire. It horrified the town. Caution was the word far and wide, and fear and terror reigned supreme. Terror-stricken parents locked up their children indoors. The children were so scared that they dreamt of nothing but ghosts and spirits and often woke up in the middle of the night screaming for help. Such was the terror!

The murder was reported to the local police. They investigated the whole matter, but were not able to find any trace of the killer. However, inquiry revealed some gripping facts. It was discovered that on the morning of the murder, Maqsood had bought a rope from Rahimullah, a local shopkeeper. He was questioned by the police but was found innocent. One resident even claimed that Maqsood was "commanded by a ghost" to fetch a rope in return for a big fortune. Some believed him, but others didn't.

The mystery remained unresolved.

The Drowning of Poor Boba

Poverty and homelessness had led many a native of Shah Sahib Bari to robbery and violence. But Boba was not among them. Poor, deaf, and dumb, he was a tall fellow of twenty-five with a distinctively dark complexion. His endurance was legendary, and he knew nothing but meditation—the art of the mystics.

In the bloody chaos of independence in 1947, Boba had lost his parents. It was then that a sense of deprivation had taken a firm root in the soil of his brain. He never recovered from that. The years of hardship that followed had a devastating effect on his mind and body, though surprisingly, he never complained.

After the partition of British India, things changed. Nizamuddin, a local building contractor who had known Boba's father well, took pity on Boba and offered him his annex, one-room quarters appended to his elegant dwelling. It was indeed a kind gesture, and Boba accepted it without a second thought. Nizamuddin, who had remarried after the death of his first wife

Roshan Begum, was known for his generosity; he was particularly generous toward Boba.

But Boba had other plans. He wanted to rely on his own strength, and he wanted to save some money and support his family as a respected member of society. It was this sense of independence and self-reliance that prompted Boba to leave Nizamuddin.

What followed was Boba's frantic search for a job. It was his firm resolve that kept him going. After countless rejections, he finally got a job at Tejgaon Jute Mill, which was owned by a local businessman. His job wasn't very appealing—separating the different types of jute—but Boba was delighted.

Tejgaon had the looks of an industrial town, although the trade units set up here from time to time were actually small and medium enterprises. The town was connected to Shah Sahib Bari by Nama Lake and was surrounded by a few rectangular, manmade ponds. One of the ponds, unlike others, was fishless and known for its "supernatural power." The natives called it *Bhoot Ghar* (House of Ghosts). After the tragic drowning of a local farmer's eight-year-old son, who knew swimming better than anything else, no one had ventured going there. Some natives believed that the ill-fated boy was gobbled up by an unknown creature living in the pond. No one had actually seen the creature, but some elders of the area seriously claimed that they had often heard its horrifying howl after sunset. Such reports, although unconfirmed, had forced the local leader to declare it a no-go area. Ignoring his warning, some natives still visited the site once in a while.

Monsoon in Tejgaon meant more trouble than joy. Heavy, incessant rains forced the people to stay indoors or travel by boat to their workplaces. Like other workers, Boba would get on a passenger boat every morning to get to the jute mill. The inconvenience of his trip every single day of the week did not bother him, for he thoroughly enjoyed the dignity of hard work. When Boba's hard work was rewarded with his monthly pay for the first time, his excitement knew no bounds. The sudden brightening of his vision, the agreeable smile on his worker's face, the profound happiness of his heart—everything was so clearly evident.

It was Boba's first pay, the fruit of his labor, the recognition of his independence. He had worked strenuously and had every reason to be happily lined up with his coworkers to collect his wages.

That particular day, it had been raining since morning, and the sky was dismally overcast. A violent storm was brewing up somewhere in the north and was predicted to strike Tejgaon shortly. When it finally did, lightning and thunder joined hands to strike fear into feeble hearts. Boba was oblivious to all this, for he heard nothing and said nothing. He was lost in his own little world of imagination, a world free of the harsh realities of life.

When the jubilant workers decided to call it a day, it had already grown dark. Everyone was in a hurry to get home, so they all rushed toward the passenger boat. No worker wanted to miss it, for it was the last boat of the day.

In the noisy run for a place on the boat no one paid attention to the sailor's warning; consequently, the boat was overloaded. Boba was slow to start, but he was able to get on the vessel seconds before the final whistle.

By that time, the winds had assumed the form of a frightening storm shaking the fragile boat on wild waters, like a bull twisting and turning his rider in a rodeo. There was no one to hear the frantic cries of the passengers when the inevitable happened: the boat capsized.

Luckily, the workers knew how to swim and all swam to the nearest edge. His wages firmly gripped in his fist, Boba drifted along cautiously. Raqeeb, his best friend at the mill, was first to get to the edge. He stood there waving and urging the others not to lose hope, but Raqeeb was a little worried about Boba, for the latter was the only deaf and dumb member of the workforce.

Raqeeb was watching Boba wrestle with turbulent waters

when, all of a sudden, he lost sight of him. There was no sign of Boba anywhere. Raqeeb moved his head frantically in all directions. He shouted "Bobaaa! Bobaaa!" at the top of his voice, but his cry was gobbled up by the storm. It only broke the spell of a barking dog in the woods. Desperate and terrified, Raqeeb raised his hands toward the heavens and prayed for a miracle to happen. It didn't. There was no sign of Boba anywhere. Poor Boba was drowned! With tearful eyes and dripping clothes and sagging spirits, Raqeeb dragged himself toward home. His home, he now felt, was farther than the farthest corners of the earth.

When the sun came out the next morning, there was no trace of the midnight madness. Everything seemed calm and normal, as if nothing had happened. The locals did report Boba's being missing to the police, who at once dispatched their divers to look for his body. It took them an hour to get to the bottom of the tragedy. All the mill workers had managed to save their own lives except Boba. Poor Boba! How come such a good swimmer gave in to the waves? No one had a clue to this puzzling question, not even the police.

Back in his quarters, the cold, rigid body of Boba lay on a wooden cot. His gleaming face told a tale of unfulfilled dreams. The smile on his face had solidified forever. Raqeeb could not control his emotions; he wept like a child and made others weep.

When the mourners began to leave one after the other, Raqeeb caught sight of Boba's right fist. It was tight and stiff, as if the fingers were glued to his palm. Raqeeb walked up to the cot and gently separated the fingers from the palm. What he saw next shocked him. A crumpled hundred-rupee note was resting on his silky palm, and it was dry. Raqeeb picked it up and unfolded it. To his utter amazement, he found a piece of hastily cut paper with a handwritten note on it: "A doll for Munni, a ring for me." The note was not signed, but it was clear who had written it.

A Safe Haven for Evil Spirits, Black Magic

Nama had always lived up to its reputation of being a sanctuary for ghosts and evil spirits. Eye-witness accounts of strange occurrences were not rare in the area. On one occasion, SAJ, SKJ, and STJ witnessed at least three alien creatures, jinn most probably, resting on top of a bamboo tree. They were small, dark, and hairless, and they resembled human beings. *"Bhaag! Bhoot! Bhoot!"* (Run! They're ghosts!) shouted SAJ. Without wasting a second, the three brothers turned back and ran as fast as they could until they got home and slammed the door behind them.

That was the brothers' last trip to Nama. "What added to the horror that day," recalls SKJ, "was that our domesticated goats, which usually grazed at Nama, came running after us as soon as we got home. When I looked out the window to see if someone was chasing the goats, I saw no one, which led me to believe that the goats too had seen the phantoms and had fled the scene for safety."

Some Nama residents also seriously believed that the jinn visited the human graves on a regular basis and fed on dead bodies and bones. There were others who believed that a beast by the name of Rackshash lived in an old abandoned house deep in the woods. They claimed that "it had eyes on both sides of the head, the front and the back, so it could see in all directions at the same time." Some residents also claimed that they had seen Rackshash mostly at night and had narrowly escaped its vicious attacks.

Demon-Possessed Nurul

Nurul, a promising Nama native, had his own tale of terror to tell. One July evening, as he was strolling up the narrow trail leading to his quarters, he spotted a headless creature dressed in black, sitting cross-legged beside an old, fruitless tree. It was a spectacle of great terror. Out of curiosity, Nurul asked him his name: "*Ei Je, tomar naam ki?*" What happened next was extremely dreadful: poor Nurul was demonized.

This terrible occurrence was confirmed by none other than Nurul's own family. They admitted that they had seen Nurul resting on the highest branch of a tree in their backyard. When they told him to come down, he started breaking the branches of the tree and throwing them at his family.

Karaar, Nurul's cousin and very close friend, was there at the time of the strange incident. He tried to climb up the tree to bring Nurul down, but was "thrown back at excessive speed by some unseen power," he said. Karaar came rolling down and hit the mud floor face down; he almost broke his ribcage. His family members, who were all there to witness the creepy incident, were stunned. Something was seriously wrong, they thought. Their fears came true when Nurul started uttering words and phrases that people normally associate with a crazy person. But Nurul wasn't crazy—he was demonized!

The news of Nurul's demonization spread like jungle fire. It gave credence to the rumors that Nama was indeed a sanctuary of jinn and evil spirits.

In the meantime, people in and around Nama started gathering at Nurul's place to lament the loss of a noble native. The *maulvis* and *aamils* (religious and spiritual practitioners), experienced in handling such cases, began their own bizarre treatment to normalize the poor soul. But they had no immediate success.

After a while, Nurul came down unassisted and was sweet-talked into a room by Karaar. The two remained in the room for some time. Then, all of a sudden, Karaar ran out of the room and locked Nurul inside. The *maulvis* and *aamils*, who had been waiting for this opportunity for a long time, started reciting verses and prayers and antidotes from the Holy Quran and other sources. After an hour or so of recitation, the demon vacated Nurul and fled the room, leaving behind a gusty current of air that almost uprooted the mud house.

Nurul's normal self was restored. His tearful parents prostrated themselves on the mud floor and thanked God for His mercy. Nurul's friends surrounded him and squeezed him tight to express their joy. It was an amazing sight!

Karaar then narrated the terror tale to Nurul, the tormenting experience the poor soul had to go through. Nurul didn't believe him but insisted that he had seen a headless creature dressed in black sitting cross-legged beside an old, fruitless tree.

The Hanging of a Poor Native Woman

Not enough is known about this Nama woman, who had reportedly committed suicide by hanging herself or was beaten to death by an unidentified assassin. Because the gruesome occurrence had surfaced about the same time Maqsood Gawala was found dead, some Nama locals believed that the two killings were somehow connected, though no one ever came up with any credible evidence.

A more puzzling detail is that this nameless woman was an outsider who was seen in the Nama village only on the day she was found dead. The few people who had a glimpse of her dreadfully stiff body described her as "a middle-aged, skinny woman with almost no flesh on her body clad in a Bangladeshi sari without a blouse."

It was also rumored that the woman was chased by a pair of evil, bloodthirsty vampires, who, upon finding her unaccompanied, sucked her to death.

The residents continued to wonder for several years after the ghastly event as to why someone would want her dead.

MOM, SSJ, Witchcraft

While demons visited Magh Bazaar once in a while, the town had its own share of strange people—the dreaded creatures who practiced the evil art of witchcraft with impunity.

One victim of their witchcraft was a woman whose real name was not known but who was always referred to as the "Mother of Mariam (MOM)." She would bear a child almost every year, whom she would always name Mariam, but for some inexplicable reason, none of the infants would survive for more than a week.

Some of MOM's sympathizers told her that the recurring tragedy was the result of some kind of *jadoo-tona* (witchcraft) or black magic. They advised her to consult a witch doctor or an *aalim* (scholar) of some repute to seek an antidote against the ill effects of the wicked spell.

The witch doctor MOM visited commanded her to fetch a bunch of nails and hair of a healthy child to perform an *amal* (act). This act, he claimed, would result in the death of the healthy child and in return enable her next child to survive.

MOM did exactly what she was told to do. To her extreme delight, her next child survived and blossomed into a tall, healthy young man.

———

Some of our own family members, according to Mother, had also been victims of the witchcraft practiced in Magh Bazaar.

I, for example, "was born with an additional finger clinging to the little finger of the left hand," Mother said. There was nothing sinister about the sixth finger, but when it was amputated, per our doctor's advice, Mother noticed a chain of "unusual things" happening to me. She noticed that I would "at times start breathing heavily, like a mill in motion, and close [my] eyes for no particular reason, or move [my] pupils up and down; and on occasion, [I] would drop [my] head on [my] left shoulder, as if lifeless." I was only two at the time.

When the same things happened over and over again, in quick succession, Mother got seriously upset and shared her worries with our next-door neighbor. The wife of Uncle Bashir, whom Mother trusted the most, told Mother in very certain terms that somebody had cast a wicked spell on me. She advised Mother to consult a witch doctor at once to get a permanent cure.

According to Mother, the witch doctor looked at my fingernails and my hair and then closed his eyes. He kept his eyes closed for a while and then opened them with a bizarre shaking movement. He told Mother that someone was indeed controlling me through the evil powers of black magic. The witch doctor prescribed some antidotes, which Mother performed as soon as she returned home. "Never again did you behave strangely in your life," Mother said. That was amazing!

Murgh-e-Musallam (Full Chicken)

In the Magh Bazaar area, Bashir Ahmad and his family were our only Urdu-speaking neighbors. They had three daughters and three sons. "Despite the boundary wall between our house and theirs," recalls STJ, "it was like two families living under one roof. We frequently crossed over to their portion, and they dropped in on us almost every day."

Being the most qualified person around and a Class I officer in the government, Father enjoyed a position of strength and respect among his neighbors near and far, including Uncle Bashir, who always looked up to Father for support and guidance. It was indeed Father's self-confidence and courage that made him do things that others only dreamed of doing, as the incident narrated below will show.

It all happened on the joyful occasion of the marriage of Uncle Bashir's eldest daughter. In those days it was customary in wedding receptions to serve food first to the groom's party as a gesture of goodwill and respect. The idea was to make sure that each member of the groom's party was sufficiently fed before the others could eat. Among the hosts, the first to eat would be the bride's party and their invitees from far off places. The next-door neighbors and close friends of the bride's family would be the last to do so.

In Uncle Bashir's case, Father was leading the host party; therefore, he and a few of his close friends were the last to sit down for dinner. To Father's great disappointment, there was nothing left to eat. By then, all the food had been consumed by the guests.

That was outrageous, in view of Father's unbearable appetite after all that waiting. Father shouted, "Serve whatever is available!" To contain Father's anger before it got out of control, someone reported that the only food left was murgh-e-musallam, a dish of full chicken with *masala* (a mixture of spices), but no rice or chapati to go with it. "*Wohi lay aao!*" (Bring that!) Father shouted. As soon as the food was served, the starving party all devoured it in a flash.

The murgh-e-musallam Father and his close friends had gulped down was actually reserved for the groom, and it was to be served to him in private. When the time came, Uncle Bashir was informed that the special dish reserved for the groom had already been served to the host team on Father's instructions.

Uncle Bashir let out an ear-splitting "What!" For a moment, the earth seemed to have slipped away from under his feet. An exchange of hot words between Uncle Bashir and Father followed, which no one had ever expected. Uncle Bashir was not ready to accept Father's clarification; Father obviously didn't know that the murgh-e-musallam was reserved for the groom. Uncle Bashir refused to budge, so the host party, led by Father, walked out of the venue in protest.

After some time, Uncle Bashir realized his mistake and arranged a separate meal for the host party, which apparently brought the two old friends back together. The whole episode left an imprint of mistrust between the two families for all time.

Siddique Kon! (Siddique? Who?)

Another horrifying aspect of living in an area populated by hostile locals was the permanent fear of being attacked or ambushed, particularly during the days of the turmoil in 1970, when the hatred against the West Pakistanis and non-Bengalis had reached its bloody climax.

However, that was not true of the entire local population, as there were many noble souls among the Bengalis who understood the gravity of the situation and were ever ready to help and guard their non-Bengali neighbors and acquaintances.

One such noble soul was Mr. Siddique, arguably the richest man in the vicinity, who disregarded the prevailing turbulence and visited our house every now and then. He would enquire about our welfare and comfort us with his presence and assurances of safety.

Although we expected Mr. Siddique almost every single day, we were never ignorant of the volatile situation gripping the area. Father always kept himself well prepared for any eventuality, keeping his hunter's rifle and other homemade weapons loaded all the time to respond to any emergency or surprise attack.

One frightful evening, just a little after sunset, someone knocked at our door two times in quick succession. Father, without showing any sign of fear, enquired in a very loud voice: "*Kon?*" (Who's that?) The visitor, without identifying himself, just replied "*Hum*" (It's me), thinking that Father would recognize his voice and let him in. But Father did not want to take a chance, so he shouted at the top of his voice, "*Hum Kon?*" (Me, who?) To this the visitor said, "Siddique." To ensure the visitor's identity, Father shouted, "*Siddique Kon?*" (Siddique? Who?) Mr. Siddique, although a regular visitor, had to introduce himself in some detail before he was allowed to enter the house.

Interestingly, while all this dialogue was going on, Father had kept his rifle ready in his hand to deal with any untoward incident, for anything was possible in those unpredictable times.

Father had a great ability to handle such situations, and it was his fearless approach that kept the miscreants at bay.

Mangtoo Phua and STJ's Lucky Escape

We called her Mangtoo Phua and without doubt she was the oldest living member of the family after *daadi* (grandmother) at the time of our migration in 1971. I was four or five when I first saw her, a sari-clad, dark-skinned lady of little height. She must have been around sixty then.

Hers was an unusual name, probably because of the symbolism attached to it. It had remained a mystery for many years until one day the riddle was sorted out by Mother: "She was named Mangtoo because her birth was the result of repeated pleas made to God by her parents. Their petitions were answered after years of wait and endurance."

According to the family tree, our grandmother and Mangtoo Phua's grandmother were sisters. At the time of fall of Dacca in 1971, Mangtoo Phua, who had been residing in Mirpur, migrated to West Pakistan along with her only son Moiz, his wife, and their two girls. They all settled in a small house in Rawalpindi. Moiz bhai soon got a job at a utility store in Rawalpindi and worked there for a few years, along with Ashfaq bhai. Then, assisted by Mazhar Chacha, our uncle, he went to Sharjah, UAE, for better livelihood and worked there for several years. Sharjah in those days was a workers' paradise following the discovery of oil in UAE in 1966.

According to SKJ, Mangtoo Phua visited our Magh Bazaar house occasionally, particularly on the *urs* (death anniversary) of Shahsahib Bari, where "she sold homemade dolls. She was a typical Bihari, not just because she had a Bihari complexion, or wore a sari 365 days a year, or chewed pan, but also because she talked and behaved and acted and reacted like a typical Bihari!"

Another thing that Mangtoo Phua did every year without fail was *Koonda*. This traditional offering, or *niaz*, is held on the twenty-second day of the Islamic month of Rajab in honor of Imam Jafar Sadiq (RA), one of the great imams of Islam. Although Father never hosted such an offering, as far as I know, he would positively respond to Mangtoo Phua's invitation and also take some of us along. We always looked forward to such visits in anticipation of a variety of delicacies: *halwa-puri, kheer, channay,* and *naan.* Father considered *Koonda* to be nothing more than a sweet tradition.

Another of Mangtoo Phua's peculiarities was that she, unlike most sub-continental Muslim women, always visited the local mosque for Friday prayers, although such visits are not mandatory for Muslim women.

At home, Mangtoo Phua's ties with her *bahoo* (daughter-in-law) were bitter all year round, with an occasional cessation of hostilities. Every now and then, Father would receive an SOS from Moiz bhai to help make peace between the two ladies. However, at the tail end of her life, when Mangtoo Phua had been bedridden at her son's apartment in Karachi for some time, her *bahoo* reportedly took good care of her.

Mangtoo Phua's ties with our family had always been good; she loved staying at our place once in a while. She was like a grandmother to us, and we visited her on a regular basis. She was around one hundred when she breathed her last.

One creepy incident, disclosed by SKJ after years of silence, featured Mangoo Phua and STJ, when he was about ten or twelve years old. "One summer evening," SKJ began, "we were on a customary visit to Mangtoo Phua's Mirpur quarters. It was a *katcha ghar* (mud house) with a *khuddi* toilet located at some distance from the living room. (The *khuddi* toilet system required squatting over one-and-a-half foot rests on either side.) After the initial exchange of greetings and pleasantries, tea and snacks were served by the hosts and thankfully consumed by us. Soon afterward, I felt the need to go to the toilet and made my intention known to Mangtoo Phua. She indicated to me where the toilet was, but before I could get there, STJ made a sudden dash in the same direction, announcing that his need was greater than mine.

"What happened next was a desperate struggle for survival, for STJ had accidentally stepped on the thin cardboard lid of a stool gutter and, ripping it, fallen straight into the filthy drain. STJ's frantic cry for help that followed silenced the conversation in the living room. We all ran toward the drain, reciting the Quranic verses that we could recall. What we saw when we got there was dreadfully disturbing: STJ had landed in waist-deep human shit! What was worse was that there were no stairs to the floor of the drain. And on top of that, it was pitch-dark in there.

"Father, who would normally keep his cool, lost his good sense for a moment that fateful day and attempted to jump into the drain. But Moiz bhai, like an angel of life, seized Father's hand and pulled him back just in time. Now the question was how to get STJ out of that horrible ditch. We all had begun to get panicky when someone, Moiz bhai probably, advised Father to drop a long rope or string into the drain for STJ to grab. Thank God, the plan worked. STJ held the rope tight and was pulled out of the drain to sighs of relief by those around.

"Then began a long cleanup operation! STJ was rushed to a bathroom, where Mangtoo Phua washed him from head to toe. Then she gave him a full body massage, for which she used the traditional mustard oil.

"Nothing but God's mercy was what saved STJ on that dreadful day!"

SKJ's Adventurism

As a young man, SKJ always boasted of his great sense of adventure, which was indeed far more developed than any of his other senses. That obviously encouraged him to pursue his various missions with impunity; however, most of his missions would end disastrously as soon as they were brought to the notice of Father. The following real-life incidents will illustrate that.

Bunking Off Taraveeh Prayers

Because of Father's strict adherence to discipline in all matters of life, it was simply not possible to rebel against him openly, but SKJ would still try to bulldoze the enforcement of such discipline through deception and trickery. During Ramadan, for example, SKJ would frequently bunk off (intentionally miss) Taraveeh prayers and get away with it. One time, his plan didn't work; consequently, he had to face the wrath of Father.

It all started with SKJ heading toward the mosque for Taraveeh prayers, at least that is what he made Father believe. Once away from the watchful eyes of Father, SKJ skillfully turned around in the direction of home, where he thought he had more important things to do, like listening to music and repeating the lyrics after the radio singers.

Assuming that Father would be busy offering his Taraveeh prayers, SKJ, upon reaching home, turned on the radio, sat near it, and closing his eyes, launched himself into his own dreamy world of amusement. He was quite oblivious to his surroundings and the sanctity of the holy month, as well as unmindful of the possibility of Father's sudden return.

SKJ was engrossed in entertaining himself when, out of the blue, a thunderous knock at the main door roused him from his sweet dream. The Taraveeh prayers were over, and Father was back home.

"*Maaray gae!*" (I'm dead!) was SKJ's instant reaction.

Interestingly, at that very instant, SKJ was busy singing a self-modified version of a popular Indian song: "*Sajan re jhoot mut bolo/Khuda ke pass jana hai/Na haathi hai na ghora hai/Wahan paidal hi jana hai.*" (Dear friend, stop telling lies/For we have to face God/And there is no elephant or horse to take us there/We have to get there on foot.) In the modified version, the one SKJ was repeating, *haathi* (elephant) was replaced by *murghi* (hen) and *ghora* (horse) was replaced by *battakh* (duck), presumably to match the local situation.

As soon as SKJ heard Father's knock at the door, he halted singing and jumped on the bed, pulling the bedcover over him. At the same time, he closed his eyes and pretended that he was fast asleep. Obviously, SKJ did not want to open the door himself.

SKJ's plan, however, didn't work. Father had already heard him. As a result, when the door was opened by Mother, SKJ had to run for his life, dancing to the tune of "Damadum Mast Qalandar."

Kite Flying and Looting

Kite-flying was an exciting pastime, almost a routine, in Magh Bazaar, though kite-looting was far more entertaining and adventurous. Since ours was a concrete house with a high, flat roof, we considered it to be very safe for flying kites and looting them.

While SKJ enjoyed the rooftop sport day in and day out, his mind would always remain occupied with inventing better ways, fair or foul, of looting kites. It was this passion of his that eventually led him to master the art of kite-looting, chiefly the art of bringing down a kite, in just a few years of relentless practice.

To achieve all that, SKJ had to bunk off school many times a month, for the only time he could practice the art was during the daytime. Practicing it in the second half of the day was simply not possible because Father was home.

Skipping school was not always possible. When it was not, all the fun activities were staged in the afternoon. But even in the afternoon it wasn't easy to indulge freely in kite-flying or -looting as Father had strictly told us—SKJ in particular—to use the afternoon time for school-related work only. To make sure that we obeyed, Father would keep a close eye on what we did or intended to do. "To make us concentrate on schoolwork," says STJ, "Father would command us to read or memorize the answers out loud. Whenever he noticed a longer-than-necessary silence, he would let out a thunderous reminder, almost a warning, that would set us all in chorus again."

During the entire study session, SKJ's attention would remain focused on the more glamorous world outside, the far more exciting world of kite-flying and kite-looting, which distracted him so much that at times he would simply scuttle to the roof to acquire firsthand knowledge of the day's events.

Once SKJ was on a routine inspection of the sky when he spotted a never-ending string (*dor* or *manja*) passing a meter or two above his head. SKJ blinked a few times to make sure that he wasn't dreaming. Of course, he was not dreaming; as a matter of fact, his dream had come true. Just then SKJ heard a painful cry. It was the poor kite-flyer whose *dor* it was. The hapless chap had just lost his kite in a midair battle and was lamenting the loss of the many meters of his precious *dor*.

That was too much of a temptation for SKJ. Without wasting any time, he leaped into the air, grabbed the *dor*, did a little dance then and there, and began pulling the *patang* (kite) down.

That wasn't good news for the ill-fated kite-flyer, who had by then realized that someone else was holding the reins of his lost investment. He sprinted as fast as he could toward the scene of the loot, where SKJ was busy wrapping up the whole operation.

Upon reaching the scene, the miserable young man pleaded with SKJ to let him have his kite and the *dor* back, but SKJ, like a gang leader of some standing, rejected his pleas.

The ensuing commotion alerted Father, and upstairs he ran to investigate. What he saw there didn't please him at all: SKJ was vociferously arguing with a street boy about a petty kite. SKJ was supposed to be indoors doing his school homework, but here he was on the rooftop, presiding over his loot.

Father's reaction was fast and furious. He commanded SKJ to return to his studies at once, but to no avail. SKJ was adamant on completing his mission. He returned to his studies only after his rooftop job was done, to his great delight.

SKJ's joy was, however, short-lived, for as soon as he returned to his studies, Father's wrathful presence greeted him. What followed was another episode of "Damadum Mast Qalandar!"

The funny side apart, SKJ's kite-flying adventures were sometimes fraught with danger. Once, he was busy looting a kite on the roof of Digha Lodge when SNJ, who was with him at the time, tripped and fell down from the roof, about a dozen feet, onto the grassy ground of the backyard. SNJ was five or six then, but fortunately he was unhurt. According to SKJ, "while I frequently jumped from the roof at the sight of Father entering the house, it was some sort of a miracle that SNJ at so young an age had remained unharmed after the fall. SNJ's fall was his very first and incredibly safe."

"Mood Nahin Hai!" (I Don't Feel Like Answering Your Question!)

As soon as SKJ graduated, Father, through one of his contacts at Heavy Foundry and Forge Ltd, Taxila, arranged a job interview for him. To make sure that SKJ passed the interview, Father decided to hold a mock interview with him, with Father acting as the interviewer and SKJ as the candidate. The idea was to test

SKJ's general knowledge and confidence and to prepare him for the real interview.

To SKJ's utter amazement, Father started the interview with a very basic question: "What is your name?" Expecting a trickier question than this, SKJ took it as an insult and refused to answer. *"Mood nahin hai,"* replied SKJ, by which he meant that he didn't feel like answering such a silly question.

While SKJ's reply produced a fair amount of laughter from SAJ and STJ, who were both watching the interview backstage, it didn't impress Father at all. To him, SKJ had not behaved again and deserved another episode of "Damadum Mast Qalandar."

A few days later, SKJ did appear for the real interview and was hired by the company. It was a great opportunity for SKJ to be associated with such a prestigious institution so early in his career.

SKJ worked at the foundry for almost a year before he got a lucrative offer from the Ministry of Defence, Sultanate of Oman, thanks once again to Father. SKJ worked in Muscat, the posh capital of the royal state, for about ten years, returning home after having amassed a large fortune.

Father Takes Charge of SKJ's Education

SKJ's addiction to extra-curricular activities, distractions, and diversions had dealt a serious blow to his studies, which became more evident when he failed twice in Class VIII, to the great embarrassment of the family. It was then that Father decided that enough was enough. It was time that he himself took charge of SKJ and prepared him for the impending matriculation exam. The school hadn't done enough to motivate SKJ or to put him back on track; therefore, SKJ could only appear as a private candidate.

The task wasn't easy at all, in view of SKJ's lack of interest in anything academic. Also, Father in the role of a teacher was unlikely to do any good to SKJ's already declining confidence. In such intricate circumstances began the extraordinary father-son relationship.

At times it generated a lot of fun and excitement. In one of the lessons, for example, SKJ was assigned to write a letter to Father, pretending that SKJ had been living in a hostel and urgently needed some cash to meet his expenses. This is what SKJ wrote:

Dear Father,
I well.
Please send money.
Your son,
Khalid Jamil.

Father read the letter from start to end and noticed that the verb "am" was missing in the first line after the salutation. It was a small mistake that Father could have overlooked and carried on, but being in a jovial mood that day, he decided to confuse SKJ. He seriously told SKJ that his sentence did not make any sense at all, for it could only be translated into *Main kuwan.* Father was intentionally translating "well" into *kuwan,* a hole drilled into the earth to obtain water, although he knew that SKJ had used the word to mean "fine." Unable to get the joke, SKJ thought that it was the missing verb "am" that had caught Father's attention. He corrected the sentence as "I am well."

But Father was not done with SKJ yet. To confuse him further, Father insisted that his sentence was still erroneous, as it could only be translated into *Main kuwan hoon (hoon* = am), and he asked SKJ to fix it again. Unaware of the game Father was playing with him, SKJ, already annoyed to capacity, amended the sentence to "I am quite well." This, to SKJ's utter frustration, Father translated as *Main bilkul kuwan hoon (bilkul*=quite).

While Father and SKJ both appeared serious during the entire session, the former by design, SAJ and STJ were finding it awfully hard to control their laughter. When the two finally burst out laughing, it further shattered SKJ's confidence. What was surprising was that it had never occurred to SKJ that his using the word "well" was absolutely correct, nor did he ever realize that Father was doing it just for fun. On the contrary, it seemed that SKJ had at one point started believing that the word "well" only meant *kuwan* and not "fine."

Father's whole initiative, as it later dawned on SKJ, was to measure his son's confidence and help raise it a bit. It was one of those rare occasions when Father used entertainment as a tool for education and training. Since SKJ was right this time, and Father was in a witty frame of mind, the situation did not call for another episode of "Damadam Mast Qalandar."

# SKJ-STJ Joint Ventures

A Profitable Investment, Funny Events

While SKJ did enjoy his solo flights for profit, he sometimes engaged STJ as his accomplice in schemes the brothers invented for the purpose of exploiting people and situations.

Credit Buying from Rahimullah

In his grown-up years, Father was extremely social. His relatives and friends, some of whom lived in faraway places, visited him on a regular basis, sometimes in groups of twos and threes. Therefore, Father had to keep an adequate supply of edibles, or at least their raw materials, at home to entertain the guests. While most edibles—*samosas*, *phulkeys*, and *pakoras* in particular—were cost-effectively prepared at home, upon the arrival of guests, some snacks, like biscuits and *nimkos*, would be fetched from a local grocery shop run by one Rahimullah.

Getting the snacks for guests was always entrusted to STJ, and, per Father's declared policy, no family member was allowed to stare at the edibles with greedy eyes or to try to steal a cracker or a piece of cake until the guests had all been served. In fact, none of us were allowed to hang around the drawing room as long as the visitors remained seated.

This did not stop us from exploring ways of laying our hands on whatever we could. It wasn't easy. The only times we could try our luck were either before the serving of refreshments or soon after the departure of guests.

Extremely unhappy with this situation, SKJ's inventive mind soon came up with a scheme that he believed had the greatest potential to succeed. According to his plan, STJ would act as the chief executor, with the additional task of reporting to SKJ. STJ would buy biscuits at Rahimullah's shop, where Father enjoyed a thirty-day credit facility. The two brothers would then meet at a specified location on the outskirts of Nama, a few hundred meters away from home. There they would quietly sit down under an old banyan tree, unpack the biscuits, and joyfully gobble them up one by one.

As predicted by SKJ, the plan got off to a splendid start. STJ started buying salty biscuits, twenty-five paisa per pack, once a week. The two brothers savored the snacks at the chosen spot. This went on for weeks and months without any family member ever knowing what the brothers were up to. Rahimullah was obviously under the illusion that the biscuits were being ordered by Father to entertain the guests. Anyway, it didn't bother Rahimullah a bit; he was making the money he always wanted to make.

Realizing that this wicked yet rewarding pursuit had remained unnoticed by Father, the brothers soon upgraded themselves by switching to the more expensive Glucose biscuits, a pack of which cost fifty paisa. This sudden doubling of the plunder was a daring development, for even a slight hint as to its existence could have triggered Father's wrath and led to another episode of "Damadam Mast Qalandar." Luckily for the brothers, the scheme remained a well-guarded secret until it was forsaken months later.

A noteworthy feature of the scheme was that SKJ, who claimed a lot of credit for being its inventor, had always had trouble treating STJ as his equal partner, arguing that "the architect of a plan in the business world always has greater rights than its executor." Although STJ never accepted SKJ's argument, he gradually learned to blackmail SKJ with a threat of disclosure. That was the only way, he says, that "I could assert myself and demand a respectable increase in my share of the booty."

Stolen Fruits Are Sweeter!

Another scheme that SKJ boasted of inventing, and for which he rightly deserved some credit, had to do with stealing fruits. Not the ones borne by our own trees, but those ripening in the neighbor's orchard.

The tool SKJ had made up for the purpose was a long bamboo stick with a homemade hook attached to its end to pull the fruits into our house. It wasn't child's play but a serious undertaking that required days of research and inspection of the site, as well as loads of endurance and absolute precision. Before the scheme could be put into action, the brothers thought it necessary to find answers to some very basic questions, like, "When do the neighbors leave their homes for work?," "What time do they return?," "What is the period of most activity?," and "What is the period of least activity?"

The answers to the above questions greatly helped the brothers plan their operation. It became clear to them that the best time for such an operation was between 1:30 p.m. and 2:30 p.m., when most of the residents routinely took a nap.

The operation was launched, and right away it bore fruit. What started as a weekly event soon became an everyday affair, with gradual improvement in the technique employed. According to STJ, "it was all masterfully done, with occasional errors of judgment that resulted in the fruit falling on the wrong side of the fence." In that case, it was STJ's duty to fetch the fallen fruit. "That again was highly dangerous, as there was always the risk of being caught in the act, which would have meant another episode of Damadam Mast Qalandar, perpetrated this time not by Father but by the next-door neighbor." Fortunately, it never happened, as STJ always managed to escape from the scene unharmed.

Arif Bhai's Funny Ways

Arif-ul-Haq, one of our intimate cousins, lived with us at Digha Lodge because Pfizer, the well-known pharmaceutical company where he worked, was located in Dhaka. In his youthful days, Arif bhai would keep himself busy in fun activities, making the most of entertaining opportunities that came his way. And there were many such opportunities.

Once, Arif bhai invented a very peculiar way of stealing sweets at a local *Milaad* function, a celebration of the birthday of Prophet Muhammad (upon whom be peace), which is supposed to be sacred. Assigned to distribute sweets to the participants of the *Milaad*, Arif bhai, clad in a typical *Milaad* dress—white *kurta, pyjama,* and *topi*—stopped where STJ was sitting and, instead of handing him just one piece of sweet as directed by the host, handed him the entire basket of sweets. This created an awkward situation for STJ, for he was not expecting Arif bhai to launch a scheme as sinful as that at such a holy gathering. Not knowing what to do, STJ quickly hid the basket behind his back and quietly disappeared from the scene. It was such a smartly executed move that no other participant ever had a clue to what the two had pulled off. SKJ, who was watching the whole operation with sweet expectations, obviously did not want to be left behind, so he quietly stood up and walked out of the room to claim his share of the loot.

Outside, without even waiting for Arif bhai to join them, the two brothers devoured the sweets one by one.

Arif bhai, whose idea it originally was, was a bit late to sneak out of the function area. By the time he joined STJ and SKJ to claim his share of the plunder, the fruit of his hard work had already been consumed by his partners. There was nothing left for poor Arif bhai. That was not so sweet of STJ and SKJ! Arif bhai had never felt as ditched as he did that particular day.

Such daredevil ventures sometimes led to funnier situations. On one occasion, Arif bhai mistook a radio *Milaad* program for a real *Milaad* gathering. He put on his *masjid wali topi* and stepped out of the house to join the assembly. When he knocked at the door of what he thought was a *Milaad*-hosting house, the hefty owner greeted him tenderly, as a neighbor would greet another, and showed him in.

There was a fairly large living room equipped with a cheap three-seat couch, a plywood dining table for eight, and a center table decorated with a white embroidered cloth.

Comfortably seated, Arif bhai moved his gaze from one corner of the room to the other, trying at the same time to overhear any *Milaad* recitation in the adjoining room. He could hear nothing but a sound like that of a radio transmission.

Oh my God! I've made a terrible mistake, thought Arif bhai, but he did not utter any word. *This is not a Milaad congregation; it's only a radio Milaad program!*

Concealing his embarrassment and telling the neighbor that he had just remembered an urgent piece of work, Arif bhai fled the scene at once.

SAJ's Admission: "I Ate the Admission Fee!"

When SAJ passed the first year of his intermediate studies at Quaid-i-Azam College, Dhaka, in 1968, it pleased Father more than anything else that year. Instantly, Father handed SAJ the admission fee for his second year of studies. SAJ grabbed the money with a broad smile on his face and ran to the college to deposit the fee.

The endless queue outside the admission office disappointed SAJ a bit, but he had no choice; like others, he could only wait for his turn, which he patiently did.

Hardly a few minutes had passed when all of a sudden a group of rowdy students at the tail of the lineup broke the queue and charged the fee clerk, yelling and swearing at him. This enraged not only the fee clerk but also the queued-up students, including

SAJ. But he kept his cool and waited for his turn, which now looked like a remote possibility.

When SAJ's turn finally came after an hour of patient waiting, he gave the clerk his name, roll number, and a few other details to get him started. Then he waited for the clerk to ask for the fee, but for some strange reason the clerk didn't. "The fee clerk simply didn't ask for the fee," SAJ said. Instead, without collecting the fee, he handed the receipt to SAJ.

SAJ bit his index finger twice to make sure that he wasn't dreaming. Of course he was not, and the fee clerk wasn't drowsy either. What was it, then, that had made the clerk so forgetful and careless? The poor man's mind was possibly so preoccupied with the disruption caused by the rowdy students that he had lost his focus.

On the other hand, the prospect of keeping the unpaid fee all to himself was challenging SAJ's conscience in a way that he had never anticipated. He stood there for some time, hoping that the clerk would somehow wake up and ask for the fee. He didn't! He simply didn't! Instead, he called, "Next."

Turning back, SAJ thought about the unpaid fee once more, telling himself that the money didn't belong to him, that he needed to give it to the clerk.

While SAJ's mind was busy dealing with the tricky situation, the Devil jumped in with a sermon on the need to keep the unclaimed money for purchases later. The Devil's sweet talk must have blurred SAJ's conscience for a moment, and it was in that one moment that SAJ quietly disappeared from the scene.

SAJ was now in possession of twenty rupees, which was considered a big amount of money those days. No wonder he was under tremendous pressure to conceal it or spend it secretly.

Despite his best efforts to hide his growing uneasiness, SAJ couldn't stop behaving strangely, which clearly showed on his face and in his actions and reactions for a whole week or so following the incident.

Then one dismal day he disclosed it all. He shared the details of that eventful day with SKJ and STJ. SAJ made it clear that he had waited for a whole week before finally declaring the money as his. "But when the clerk didn't ask for the fee," he said, "I thought I had earned the right to spend the money the way I liked."

But spending such a big amount of money in a small neighborhood, away from the searching eyes of STJ, SKJ, and the other family members, wasn't easy. SAJ had come up with a solution of his own: spend part of the money at college recess time and part of it in the adjoining commercial area, some two hundred meters away from our Digha Lodge residence.

SAJ's plan would have gone smoothly had it not caught the attention of SKJ and STJ. The two had been observing the unusual behavior of their elder brother for some time and one day followed him secretly to the very restaurant where he had started spending his evenings lately. Without a second thought, STJ and SKJ raided the place and caught SAJ red-handed. "He was busy enjoying a full plate of *jalebi* and *seekh kabab* while listening to Indian movie songs!", revealed SKJ.

"What are you doing here?" was SKJ's instant reaction. "How come you're eating these delicacies, and we don't know anything about it? Where did you get the money from?"

The volley of questions stunned SAJ and somewhat embarrassed him. The cat was out of the bag, which meant that SAJ now had no choice but to reveal the secret. STJ and SKJ instantly demanded their share of the ill-gotten gains in exchange for not disclosing it to anyone else. SAJ had no option but to succumb to their demand.

The three brothers then made the most of the remaining cash, stuffing their bellies with *seekh kabab, jalebi, dahi-bundia, rasgullah,* and *chena badaam* for a number of days thereafter. "The delicacies weren't at all expensive. That is why we were able to relish them for so many days without anybody noticing it!", remembers STJ.

# Trip to India

SAJ, SKJ, AND STJ OCCASIONALLY SING praises of a very entertaining visit to India in 1961, a few years before the first bloody conflict between Pakistan and India. The key purpose of the visit was to see our maternal grandparents and to spend some time in Digha Ghaat, where Father had spent his early childhood.

It was the brothers' first-ever journey by train in the delightful company of Mother, Uncle Seraj, and his sons, Inam, Qayam, and Minhaj, the last three our cousins.

The vacationers were so excited and thrilled during the course of the trip that they all kept smiling and laughing and cutting jokes and looking out the train windows and making a running commentary of the outing and the sights and sounds they came across, without once feeling the need to rest or take a nap. Such was the adventure and the excitement!

This incredible merrymaking was briefly interrupted by the sudden entry of a train onto the Hooghly Nadi Bridge with a deafening roar, thanks to the heavy steel structure on both sides of the bridge. It frightened every one of the travelers, and Qayam bhai even shouted "Sher Aagaya!" meaning "A tiger has attacked!"

What followed was a sudden hush over the entire group, as every member uneasily waited for the train to outrun the bridge. As soon as it did so, everything—the thrill, the excitement, the merrymaking—picked up again.

At the crack of dawn the following day, the train halted for the first time, and Inam bhai shouted "Kulkatta Aagaya!" They were now in the city of Calcutta (Kolkata). SAJ stood up, lifted his arms, and peered out the window, making his own little announcement: "No more twisting of the ears and lifting of the body to see Kulkatta. It's right here, before our very eyes!"

The Calcutta railway platform was a picture of great joy and wonder: the hustle and bustle of the cultural metropolis, the many different sounds originating from the nooks and corners, the earsplitting calls for *naashta, halva poori, pakwan, chai*, and whatnot. Regrettably, no one was allowed to get off the train; the instructions to remain seated were strict.

SAJ, the senior-most among the boys, wasn't happy about the restriction at all. He, as well as the others, was desperate to get off the train to feel the typical essence of the city, its many sights and sounds, and the warmth of the people in the street. The frown on SAJ's face clearly depicted his frustration. He finally vented his anger by teasing a platform hawker. He made faces and produced a sarcastic grin, something he had never done before. "The poor hawker got so mad that he approached SAJ, presumably to beat him up, but luckily, the railway guard blew the whistle about the same time. The train kicked in and soon picked up speed.", reports STJ.

The next station was Patna, the capital of Bihar, the family's home province. Here the group split into two parties. The one led by Mother headed toward Sharfuddinpur, Mother's ancestral village. The other led by Uncle Seraj hit the road to Digha Ghaat Haveli. It was a temporary split; the first party, after spending about two weeks in Sharfuddinpur in the soothing company of maternal grandparents and cousins, rejoined the second party in Digha Ghaat Haveli.

A pleasant welcome and a whole bunch of surprises awaited the merrymakers as they arrived in Sharfuddinpur, just about noon.

The first surprise upon reaching destination was a plate of round biscuits, also called "Larva Biscuits," a kind of rusk popular in those days. "It was amazing to see so many of them. We had never come across such abundance in Magh Bazaar.", recalls STJ.

This was followed by a plate of yummy *maleedah—roti* pieces mixed with *ghee* and *shakkar*.

The biggest surprise came a few hours later when some members of the group felt the need to go to the toilet. To their utter shock, they were told that no men's room existed in the house. The only thing they could possibly do was grab a *badhna* (a toilet water container) and walk to the nearby woods to relieve themselves.

When the male members of the group did reluctantly go out holding *badhna* in their hands, another surprise awaited them in the woods: quite a few people were already there, busy in various stages of relieving themselves. Most of these people had successfully camouflaged themselves, but a few were clearly visible. Not groomed for such an eventuality, the visitors confronted it as a great challenge, one that they would never forget. No one could reconcile to the idea that such a thing still existed in the village.

There was nothing they could do about it. It soon became a routine, a common sight, a filthy necessity. Time and again someone would bump into a fellow-being on his way to the "open air toilet." The mere thought of somebody appearing at the site at the wrong time was disturbing. "However, to avoid any awkward situation, we gradually learnt to finish the whole act speedily. Since it had become a daily occurrence in the village, the natives were quite used to it, and they never seemed rattled by it in any way.", remarks STJ.

The rest of the happenings in the village were a great source of enjoyment and learning. Besides other things, the boys also learned about a fascinating local tradition, that of nicknaming of people after the day they are born: Sanicherwa (a male child born on Sanicher, or Saturday); Mangalwa (a male child born on Mangal, or Tuesday); Budhwa (a male child born on Budh, or Wednesday); Jumaratin (a female child born on Jumarat, or Thursday).

Some other interesting events that happened about the same

time included SKJ's Hindu haircut, nilgai hunting, *gurh*-making, potato pulling, and fruit stealing.

SKJ's Hindu Haircut

Sharfuddinpur in the 1960s was inhabited by a mix of Muslims and Hindus, the former maintaining a thin majority. This slight numerical advantage did not tempt the Muslims to provoke their Hindu neighbors; instead, the Muslims carefully avoided certain acts permissible to them but not liked or approved by the Hindus, all in the spirit of brotherhood. Most of the rituals and ceremonies staged in the neighborhood were carried out with mutual consent.

One rare incident, perhaps the most hilarious of the India trip, involved SKJ, who had his hair cut by a Hindu *nai* (haircutter) in a clear case of misunderstanding. When SKJ got home, he had a ponytail prominently positioned on his head, a typical Hindu symbol. It infuriated grandmother so much that without letting SKJ take the post-haircut shower, she commanded someone to chop off the ponytail at once! The laughter that it produced was heard in the remote fringes of the region.

Nilgai Hunting

Another memorable experience the travelers went through involved *nilgai,* a cow-like animal that has the face of a horse. But it is neither a cow nor a horse; it is an antelope. It lives in the woods and sugarcane fields, and it's a common sight in many parts of India, including Sharfuddinpur.

Because of its resemblance to a cow, a *nilgai* is held in high esteem by many devout Hindus. In the decade of the 60s, the Muslims living in Sharfuddinpur were bound by an agreement with the local Hindus that allowed the former to hunt no more than one *nilgai* every week. As the Hindus considered the animal sacred and did not consume meat, all hunting was carried out indoors by a chosen group of hunters.

The village kids took great interest in the hunting process, and so did the young members of the touring party, most of whom had never seen the creature before. Since grandmother's family enjoyed a good reputation in the area, the visitors were allowed to accompany the elders to the hunting missions.

Besides being very entertaining, the hunting campaigns also considerably broadened the knowledge base of the visitors. According to STJ, one of the things the boys learned during this particular trip was that "a *nilgai* has the habit of running straight, and if you see it coming toward you, just make a swift right or left turn to avoid the deadly hit." Moreover, hunting *nilgai* didn't involve shooting of the animal with a rifle or gun, but rather spotting the animal, surrounding it, and seizing it alive. Three to four people of above-average strength were required. Once seized, the animal was dragged into a house, where it was slaughtered in the Islamic manner. The skin was removed first, and then the meat was chopped into smaller pieces and distributed among the Muslim residents of the village. Those visiting the village for the first time were given an extra piece of meat as a tourist bonus.

Gurh-Making

Another activity that the brothers and their cousins greatly enjoyed being part of was the *gurh*-making process, in which a large amount of sugarcane juice is boiled and stirred for hours to make a honey-brown sweet product called *gurh*. The whole process is completed in the sugarcane fields.

While there was no restriction on watching the process, no one was allowed to steal the finished product. Although the local villagers were permitted to take some sugarcane home, as per quota regulations in force, most of the sugarcane crop was uprooted and squeezed to make *gurh*. Those present on the occasion, the workers and the spectators, would each receive a sugarcane stalk to take home.

During one of the trips, SAJ, claiming to be senior, was able to get an extra stalk. His joy was short-lived, as he was soon spotted by one Huqqa Uncle—a hookah addict—who was considered an authority in the village. He stopped SAJ just as the latter was leaving the field, but when SAJ insisted that he had been visiting his grandmother and therefore deserved an extra stalk, Huqqa Uncle let him go.

The making of *gurh* was a day-long activity marked by crushing and squeezing of the canes. A wooden unit equipped with a pair of cows and a lever was used to crush the stalks. One or two men pushed the cows in a circle in anticipation of a big lump of *gurh*, the size of a fist, for each thirty minutes of toiling. STJ and SAJ and a few others of the touring party also took turns driving the cows, something they had not done before, to earn at least four lumps of *gurh* each.

The crushing and squeezing went on for hours and produced a greenish-yellow juice, which was poured into a very large concave pan called *karahi* that sat on top of a large burning platform. A few stout men clad in *dhoti* continuously stirred the juice with long spoons called *karchul*. The liquid was boiled for several hours until it took the form of a brown, sweet-smelling paste.

The final product, fresh and hot, was something the boys had never tasted before. According to STJ, "We hadn't tasted anything like it since we first tasted it in Sharfuddinpur. That taste has been with us since then, not on our tongues, but in our minds. The only *gurh* that matches it, to a great extent, is the Batali *gurh* we had tasted in Dhaka. What we have these days in Punjab and Sindh, unfortunately, is of a pathetically poor quality."

Potato Pulling

Another joyful experience the brothers and their cousins never tire of relating was the uprooting of ready potatoes in the lush green backyard of Grandmother's Hindu neighbor. The neighbor, Ram Mohan, apparently did not object to it, though he never seemed very happy about the "level of regularity with which we did the stealing."

SKJ, in particular, was very good at it, and it was he who had once found "the biggest potato," which he proclaimed to be his. Quickly he was made to realize that it was a group venture with equal profit and loss sharing, which meant that every participating member deserved an equal share.

Once uprooted, the potatoes were baked on the kitchen stove, and the baked potatoes were sprinkled with salt and gobbled up in no time. "It was fun of the coziest kind that made our winters so fabulous!", remembers SKJ.

More Fruit Stealing, the Haveli, the Trip Back Home

SKJ and his cousin nicknamed Patalka, a wafer-thin fellow in his teens, occasionally ventured into the fenced acres of the neighbors to steal guava, a fruit SKJ cherished the most. After a few failed attempts, SKJ's inventive mind came up with the idea of widening the space between a pair of rails of the fences for Patalka to slip through to the other side. The owner of the orchard, Sanicher Bhayya, once or twice lodged a complaint with Grandmother, but that did not have any significant effect on SKJ. The venture continued unabated, with gradual improvement in the technique employed by the two.

The trouble with good times is that they fade away quickly, without letting the beneficiaries fully relish them. This was what the touring party had to face when their journey came to an abrupt end. The visitors just couldn't reconcile to the idea of leaving Sharfuddinpur, a place that had given them so much in so little time.

The tourists' next stopover, Digha Ghaat Haveli, was equally engaging. It was where Father had spent the most beautiful days of his boyhood. The Haveli was a large square-shaped, double-story building with a spacious verandah in the middle and bedrooms on all sides. At least four joint families were living there at the time of the visit.

"It was great fun to be there!" SKJ said. As usual, he was quick to resume his bubbly activities, and he soon made friends with Tunno and Ejaz, sons of Auntie Saeeda. Together they injected a new life into the dull proceedings at the Haveli. Playing indoor games, *lattoo*, and hide-and-seek soon became the order of the day, with SKJ assuming a leadership role.

The upper story of the Haveli was occupied by a ghost, so it was labeled a no-go area for all. Everybody except SKJ believed it to be true. Curious to know the secret, SKJ made it his mission to enter the forbidden area during a hide-and-seek game. Unfortunately, his plans were made known to the family elders, who made it absolutely clear to him that such a quest "might let loose an endless chain of strange happenings." This stern warning by Auntie Saeeda stopped SKJ from approaching the area.

Thank God, no strange thing ever happened. The ghost story remained a mystery, and except for a few inexplicable rattling sounds and whispers, not one member of the touring party ever encountered a spirit or phantom.

The good days of joy and fun finally came to a close, leaving behind a rich collection of sweet memories: the joyful journey, the bliss of company, the fun, the excitement, the probing visits, the welcoming nooks and corners of the ancestral villages, and above all the meaningful interactions with grandparents and innocent villagers. The sudden awareness that the trip had come to an end saddened the boys for a while. The knowledge that they were bound for Dhaka now cheered them up again. In Dhaka, *daadi* and Father would be eagerly waiting to embrace them.

Father, the only civilian in the picture, with his CENTO
colleagues in Ankara, Turkey

Heading Pakistan delegation to China, Father signing
an agreement between the two countries along with his
Chinese counterpart near the Pak-China border

Father, Aapa, Mother in Lahore

Father
with a friend
on a trip

Father,
Mother at
Abdullah's
birthday

(R-L) SSJ, Father, Mother, Tahir, Shahina, and Farhat, at a park in Ankara, Turkey

Father (L) and STJ at our Rawalpindi house

Father (R)
and
Mushtaq Chacha
at our
20-A/1 residence

Mother holding Ayesha, beside Naureen in Islamabad

Mother with Shahina in Rawalpindi

Mother with Maryam

SAJ in USA

SAJ (R) and STJ (L) in a happy mood somewhere in Swat, Pakistan

SKJ at an airbase in Oman

SKJ in his Karachi office

SKJ and Tahir in a pleasant mood

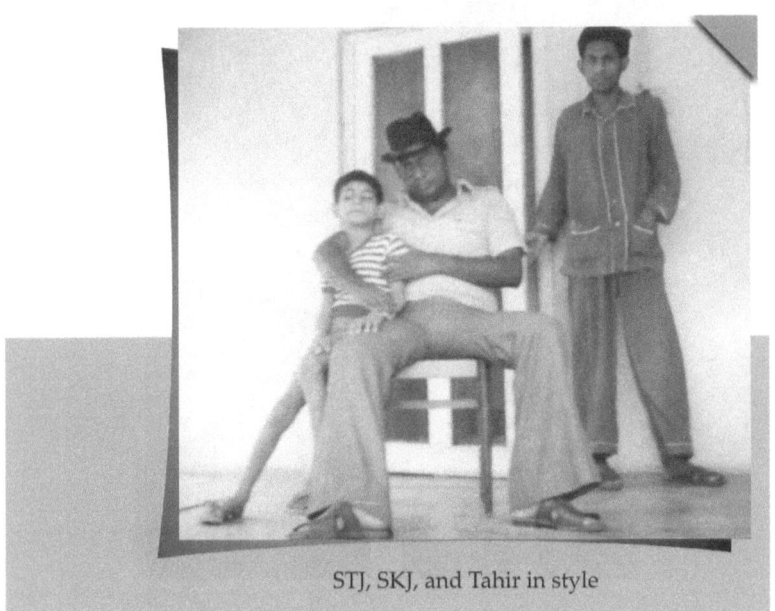

STJ, SKJ, and Tahir in style

Zarrin Khalid, SKJ's wife and our bhabi

Zaid Bin Khalid,   Faiz Bin Khalid,
SKJ's elder son   SKJ's younger son

STJ and his family (Maryam, Muniba, and Raana bhabi)

Maryam,
about 2, in Islamabad

Ali Azam (Azam bhai) in his Islamabad house

Musarrat Azam (Baji)
dressed as a pathani

Arsalan giving first driving lessons
to Sundus in Islamabad

Richmond, Canada: Ayesha cutting her 3rd birthday cake
in the presence of Talat, Naureen, SSJ, and Shahbaz

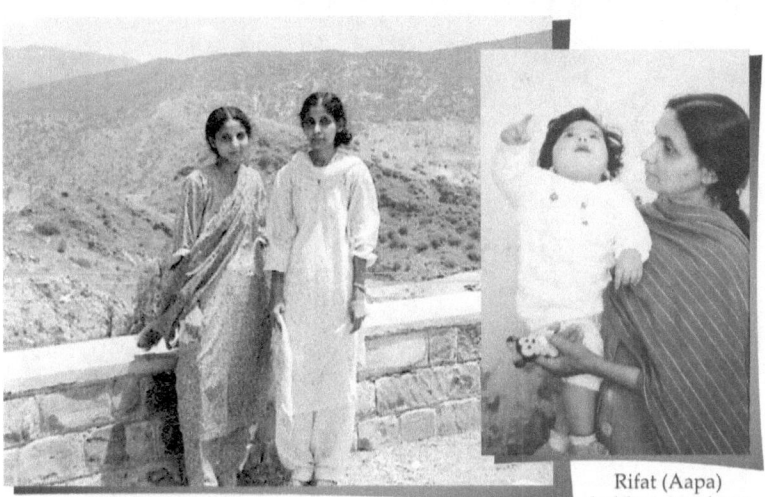

Baji and Talat somewhere in Islamabad

Rifat (Aapa)
holding Ayesha at
our Islamabad house

SNJ's family: SNJ, Sabih, Abdullah, and Seema

Tahir clinging on to SNJ
at our 4-A residence

Waheed bhai holding Ayesha
at our Islamabad house

(2nd row) SSJ (R) and Farhat (L) in their
school classroom in Ankara, Turkey

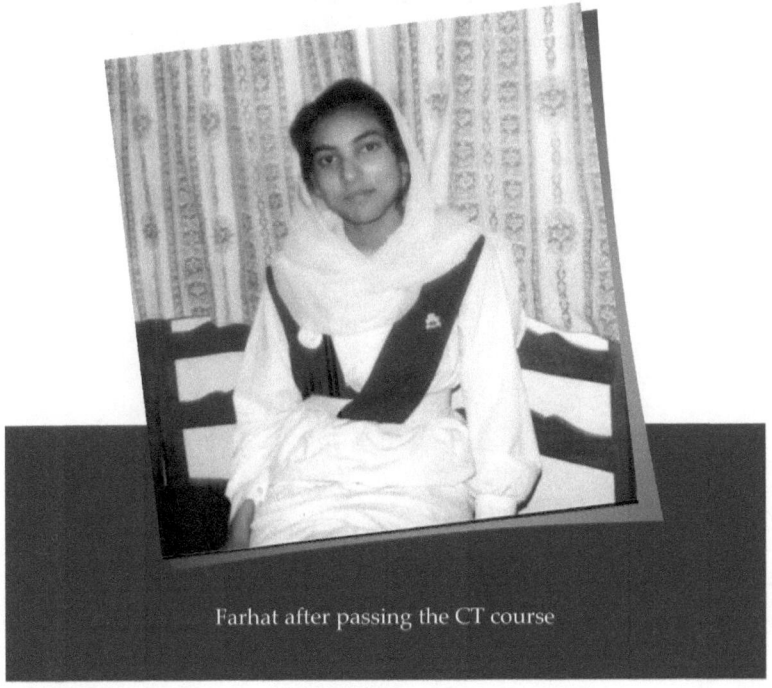

Farhat after passing the CT course

SSJ and Ayesha in Surrey, Canada

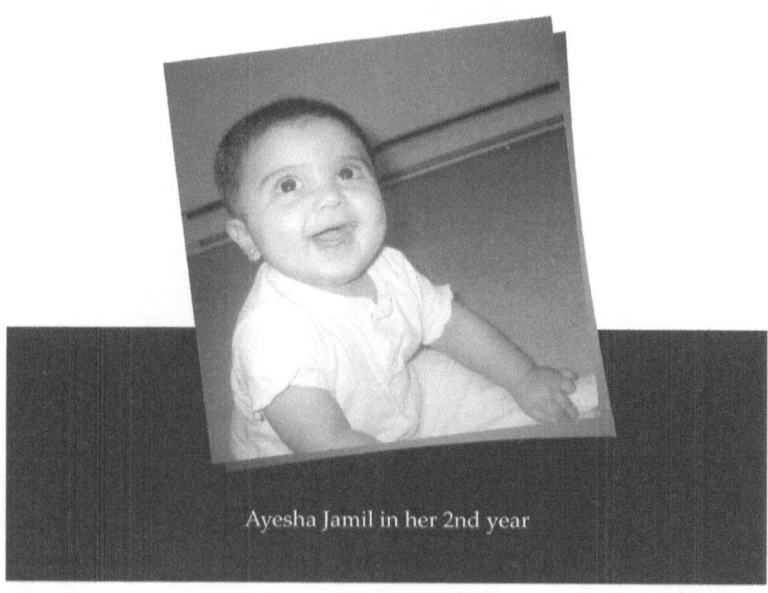

Ayesha Jamil in her 2nd year

SSJ carrying
a triumphant
Tahir on his back
in Rawalpindi.

SSJ with his
classmate Noman
in Ankara, Turkey.

SSJ with his classmate Karem Basul in Ankara, Turkey.

(Sitting R-L) Asad, Rida, Mahroo, Aashir, Tahir. (Standing R-L) Shahbaz, Arsalan, Waheed bhai, SSJ, with Ayesha, Farhat, Talat, Baji, at Naureen Dam, Islamabad Khanpur Dam, Islamabad

SAJ (L) and Ashfaq bhai on a
boating trip in Islamabad, Pakistan

SAJ inside a cave somewhere in USA.

Father at 183-D, Rawalpindi

Azam bhai's daughter
Sundus Ali and son
Asad Ali in their
Islamabad house.

Shahina on the roof of our Rawalpindi residence

SAJ-STJ Ventures

SAJ and STJ in Lahore: Injustice Triggers Revenge

Toward the end of 1971, soon after migrating from Sylhet Medical College, East Pakistan, in not so agreeable circumstances, SAJ got himself admitted to the MBBS program at the reputable King Edward Medical College, Lahore. Initially, he stayed with Uncle Ziauddin, a fast friend of Father's, before moving to the Broom Hostel of the college. In November 1973, STJ also moved to Lahore to join the equally esteemed Hailey College of Commerce for his graduate studies. To begin with, STJ also stayed with Uncle Ziauddin before moving to the college hostel.

To Father, working as a Grade-17 section officer, it was a huge financial challenge but one that he was ready to confront with a cheerful face. For obvious reasons, the financial support the two brothers did receive from Father was just enough to meet their basic needs, chiefly their educational expenses, with almost nothing for entertainment. Nevertheless, like well-bred gentlemen, the two never cried foul or shared their tight situation with anyone; rather, they made the most of what their destinies had earmarked for them.

Once in Lahore, the brothers clearly understood their objective, which was to remain focused on their studies. They had no choice but to heed Father's repeated warning against not getting a good degree. "Life without a good degree," maintained Father, "is no better than selling *chena badaam* (nuts)."

Although the brothers remained glued to their textbooks all year round, they did occasionally find time for fun together. The fun activities were, however, restricted to visiting parks, munching roadside *samosas* a few times a week, watching movies in the lower class once a month, and going window shopping on the mall every week.

In Lahore, Indian movies were a major attraction for SAJ and STJ. The rooftop antenna of the hostel TV was quick to receive Indian TV signals from across the border. At times, however, the signals weren't strong enough, so one of the hostel boys would climb the roof and readjust the direction of the antenna.

Since this was entertainment at no cost, the Indian movies quickly engulfed the entire hostel population. A lot of excitement was generated when such great stars of the time as Dilip Kumar, Ashok Kumar, Saira Bano, and Sharmila Tagore started featuring in the movies.

The brothers' occasional viewing of Indian movies, however, did not in any way weaken their resolve to concentrate on studies. They stayed focused, for that was the only option they had: "We certainly had no plans of selling *chena badaam* for a living!", recollects STJ.

Theft of the Only Trousers

During their stay in Lahore, SAJ and STJ were subjected to some real tests of patience and endurance. The following are some of the most memorable ones that still evoke laughter.

Father's tight financial situation never allowed any of his children to possess more than two sets of school uniforms at a time. SAJ, despite being the eldest, was no exception: he too had just one pair of trousers and as many shirts when he moved to Lahore to study medicine.

Mindful of his poverty, SAJ took great care of his clothes and kept them in excellent condition. But he could only delay their wear and tear, not prevent it; as a result, one of his pairs of trousers gradually faded. Now he was left with only a pair.

Luckily for SAJ, during his subsequent visit to Rawalpindi,

Father bought him a piece of cloth for a new pair of trousers. SAJ's delight was evident; he decided to get it tailored in Lahore, for stitching was cheaper there.

Upon his return to Lahore, SAJ got busy with his endless medical studies, which did not spare him any time for a visit to the tailor. Consequently, the cloth that Father had bought him in Rawalpindi remained folded in his big steel trunk, and he continued to wear his only trousers seven days a week.

Summer that year came with an overdose of heat and discomfort; as a side effect, the extreme laziness that it produced hung around for a number of days. It didn't really bother SAJ, since he literally had no time to reflect on the changing weather or the season itself. For him it was medicine not three times a day, but twenty-four hours a day. No wonder he forgot that he was living with just one pair of trousers.

Then one fine morning, the unpleasant happened. SAJ was having breakfast in the dining hall of the hostel when word reached him that some strange sounds were emanating from his room, suggesting the presence of a thief. SAJ dropped the spoon on his plate and ran to the crime scene, only to discover that his one pair of trousers was missing. They had been stolen! Not only that, the piece of cloth that Father had bought him in Rawalpindi was missing too. Someone, most probably a classmate of SAJ's, had sneaked into his room through the window and stolen his most valuable possessions. Luckily, SAJ's costly medical books remained, which saved him from going *ghola* (crazy)!

"What am I going to do now? I had just one pair and that is gone. The cloth piece too is stolen. What am I going to wear to college?" SAJ was quick to raise these critical questions, but he had no answers to them. He walked back and forth, from one end of the room to the other, head down, pondering, murmuring. After a few minutes, he suddenly stopped. He had found a short-term solution: since he didn't have anything presentable to wear that day, he would just skip college, breaking his own flawless record of attendance.

Thus, all through the day, SAJ remained locked up in his room, desperately waiting for the sun to disappear, for only then could he put on his old, worn-out trousers he had almost discarded a month ago, and quietly walk out of the hostel premises to plan a strategy for the next day. His idea made sense. As the twilight turned into complete darkness, a worried-looking SAJ, dressed in his old trousers, silently sneaked into STJ's hostel room at the New Campus of Punjab University. He was counting on STJ for a solution to this sticky situation.

STJ was in his room trying to solve an audit question when SAJ stepped in with worry writ large on his face. The latter was much relieved to see STJ and, without waiting for his breath to normalize, narrated his woeful tale to him. Although it was a pretty serious matter, the two brothers found parts of it rather amusing.

Like a considerate younger brother, STJ was quick to offer him a pair of his own trousers. But the trouble was their waist sizes didn't match. "What now?" asked SAJ. "Find a tailor," replied STJ, which they did.

The tailor they eventually found said no at first, for he needed at least a day to widen the waist. But SAJ had just a few hours at his disposal. The two students pleaded with the tailor, telling him how important it was for SAJ to attend college the following day and how important it was for the country to have more doctors. The tailor's patriotic spirit was awakened, and he cooperated. The nightmare was over.

Relieved, the two brothers thanked God for His timely help, and, instead of strolling back to their respective rooms, they decided to visit Uncle Ziauddin, their old benefactor in Lahore.

Uncle Ziauddin was as hospitable as he had always been. It was not just the sumptuous dinner that he would serve SAJ and STJ whenever the two visited him but also the great pleasure of his company, his funny tales and jokes, and his words of wisdom that continued to inspire the brothers during their stay in Lahore and long thereafter.

Small Egg Grievance

Hailing from East Pakistan, the lost wing, SAJ had gone through a terrible period dealing with the locals in the west, who openly discriminated against him for being an emigrant from what they called the "mutinous" east. Despite that, SAJ had always kept his cool and avoided confrontation, for his only aim was to complete his medical education without any disruption. Therefore, the menacing presence of a few "sons of the soil" around him did not undermine his commitment to studies. Above all, he never disregarded the fact that he belonged to a very noble family, which called for a particularly refined behavior, more so in times of crisis.

But there is a limit to what a man can tolerate! The discriminatory treatment that SAJ received at King Edward Medical College (KEMC) was a dirty trick employed not only by his classmates but also by some hostel employees.

One such case of discrimination involved a waiter whose grudge against SAJ was common knowledge. SAJ, like many other resident students, used to eat his morning meal in the breakfast room of the hostel. As days passed, he began to notice that whenever he sat down to eat, the waiter on duty ignored and delayed his orders. SAJ soon got the impression that the waiter was doing it on purpose. In fact, SAJ was able to gather some concrete evidence to support his claim. To his great shock, SAJ discovered that the eggs served to him by this particular waiter were always smaller in size compared with the ones served to the "sons of the soil."

It was the most outrageous form of discrimination SAJ had ever come across. Over a period of time, this sense of discrimination impacted his mind, heart, and soul so much that he eventually lost hope in the social system as a whole and instead developed a sort of hatred for the very institution that he thought was supposed to make better human beings.

This hatred came to light when time came for SAJ to leave

the college hostel. At that time, instead of getting the mandatory clearance certificate from the breakfast room manager, SAJ signed the clearance himself and got away with it. It was obviously an act of revenge, something that clearly contradicted SAJ's own principles of social behavior. He had no regrets then, but as time passed, he began to realize the impulsiveness and unfairness of his deed on that significant day of his life. He just couldn't believe it.

Looting Strategy at Annual Functions

Except for a few lapses, SAJ has always lived up to his reputation of being a thorough gentleman and a respecter of the laws of the land. Even during the turbulent college years, he had always exhibited commendable behavior and manners. Whether it was walking on the road, or boarding the college bus, or buying a movie ticket, he would never compromise the principles of good conduct.

SAJ held on to these principles rather strictly when he attended the first annual function of KEMC since his admission to the college. He keenly listened to the customary speeches and prize announcements and remained seated until the invitees had been directed to the dining hall for refreshments. SAJ was in no hurry to get to the hall. He strolled leisurely behind the long line of the invitees. However, as soon as he entered the hall, he noticed that all the choicest items of food had already vanished: roasted chicken legs, pastries, patties, and bananas were nowhere to be found. They'd all been gobbled up in seconds. All that was left was the mouthwatering aroma of the freshly consumed foods and some leftovers. A dejected SAJ had to struggle a great deal to snatch a few bits and pieces of food.

It was unbelievable! It wasn't easy for a cultured soul like SAJ to accept what had happened. He had been expecting people to behave, but they hadn't. The incident not only awakened him to a bitter reality—the fragility of people's moral fiber—but it also shattered his belief in the civic society as a whole.

A year later, when the second annual function was announced, SAJ had the benefit of the presence of STJ, who was in Lahore to commence his studies at the Hailey College of Commerce. Without a second thought, SAJ invited STJ to attend the function as a guest. In fact, he wanted his younger brother not just for company but also for his possible help in executing SAJ's plan to make up for the 'famine' he had faced the previous year.

To start with, SAJ briefed STJ on what the former had to go through the previous year, the hideous greed and indiscipline of the participants. To express his anger in a big way, SAJ had devised a strategy to ransack the maximum this year. To make it foolproof, the brothers reflected on each step of the looting strategy before agreeing to implement it.

To make sure that the plan achieved its desired objective, the brothers began with their own secret survey of the function hall, the corridor leading to it, the likely position of tables and seating arrangements, and so forth. This was followed by a mock rehearsal a week prior to the function day.

The big day dawned with its usual excitement and thrill. Like the previous year, it was again a testing time for the members of the function committee. Soon they took up the difficult tasks of building the stage, finalizing the seating arrangements, and reconfirming the order for refreshments.

The invitees started pouring in one after the other, followed by the arrival of special guests and the chief guest. When everyone was seated, the initial formalities were carried out, which again included, to most people's dismay, some long and boring speeches. Finally, the prizes were announced for outstanding students.

As the time for refreshments approached, SAJ and STJ, who hadn't been paying attention to the useless speeches or the prize announcements, exchanged eye signals, turned about, and hurried toward the dining hall. There they took their positions by the entrance, ready to dash into the hall with the announcement for tea.

When the announcement was finally made, the brothers were the first to enter the hall and savor the appetizing aroma of the delicacies so neatly placed on the tables. Without caring in the least for the guests, SAJ and STJ started picking up the food—as many chicken legs, patties, and bananas as they possibly could, without any break. When their pockets and hands couldn't take any more, the brothers quietly walked out of the hall to a secure spot where, between bouts of laughter, they munched their loot in relative peace. The operation was a great success!

STJ's Own Exploits in Lahore

For STJ, hostel life was a unique experience, one that he still cherishes as the most eventful period of his bachelor life. But it didn't have a dream start.

Due to the late departure of the outgoing students, ten lucky newcomers awaiting allotment of rooms in the Hailey College Hostel were allowed to occupy the common room (CR) of the hostel temporarily. STJ was one of them. When STJ heard the news of his inclusion, he rushed to the hostel. There, to his utter dismay, he was told that no vacant bed was available for him; all the beds had already been taken by the other students. That prompted STJ to meet the hostel warden at once to seek his help.

The warden sounded helpless and repeated what STJ had already heard: "There is no spare bed available." STJ told the warden in very clear terms that since he himself was one of the top students on the merit list, the hostel administration needed to make some arrangements without further delay to accommodate him. The warden was convinced and offered STJ one of his own beds.

The warden's own bed was in excellent condition. STJ lifted it and carried it to the CR with a big smile on his face. When he got there, however, he discovered that the four walls of the CR, the coveted spots, had already been occupied by students from such regions of the Punjab as Lala Musa, Sahiwal, Mandi Bahauddin, and Wah Cantt. The only vacant spot available was the center. After a few moments of hesitation, STJ laid his bed right there, in the center of the CR, which raised quite a few eyebrows.

STJ's next immediate concern was to get hold of a bed sheet. Since he didn't have one, he borrowed it from SAJ. The bed sheet gave STJ a sense of ownership, which was vital in view of the lack of space and material in the college hostel.

The bed sheet laid out, STJ sprinted to fetch his luggage from Uncle Ziauddin's house. When STJ returned to the CR an hour or so later, he found that his bed, so painfully earned, was missing and a worn-out broken frame was in its place. Clearly, one of the CR occupants was behind this horrendous joke. Surprisingly, however, the bed sheet was still there, or it had been purposely left there to conceal the broken frame underneath.

An utterly outrageous act it was!

It gave STJ all the reasons in the world to yell at the occupants of the CR, each one of them, for they had all witnessed the crime as it was being perpetrated and had done nothing to prevent it. Then came STJ's stern warning: "Return my bed now, whoever has it under his ass, or be ready to face the warden's wrath!"

No one came forward to confess. They all denied having any knowledge of the mischievous act. Some of them even swore by God to prove their innocence.

STJ then approached the warden and lodged a complaint with him. That did not produce any result either. The warden didn't seem to have enough grey matter to get things done quickly.

Having exhausted all the options, STJ finally decided to lie down on the broken bed, unwillingly of course, until rooms were allotted some thirty days later.

The room allotment system at the Hailey College was one of a kind. It provided STJ with a chance to become the most sought-after student in the college, a status he exploited later on to avenge his earlier mistreatment in the common room. The allotment system was such that the rooms, each spacious enough to lodge five students, were allotted by order of merit to top twenty-five students, who were also given the right to select their four roommates. STJ was third on the merit list.

Since the common room incident was still very fresh in his mind, STJ initially decided not to select any student from the CR. It was only after the persistent pleas of the warden that STJ agreed to select four students who he thought were better than the others. Two of them were from Rawalpindi, one from Sialkot, and one from Karachi.

In fact, it was the Sialkot guy who had helped STJ select the other three. Khalid Hannan was his name, and his family was settled in Karachi for economic reasons. He was in Lahore only for his graduation.

Hannan was unique in many ways. He was extremely talkative and instantly availed of any leg-pulling opportunity that came his way. At the same time, he would beg for mercy as soon as the victim retaliated. Another of Khalid Hannan's personal traits was his overconfidence, a kind of *tandeli* that almost always bordered on arrogance. For instance, Khalid Hannan was not happy at all about STJ giving extra time to economics, a subject Hannan thought was to be studied "just like a novel, not to be taken seriously." This conviction of his made STJ and his other roommates envy Hannan's "depth" of knowledge of the subject.

Knowledge it was not, for Hannan failed economics twice and had to forego the subject altogether for the easier BA course. STJ, who had not studied the subject as a novel, got about 54 percent, beyond all expectations, including his own.

Another hostel event that STJ still remembers was the leaking out of the accounting paper, which was, no doubt, a shocking occurrence—something STJ had only heard about. Since STJ was known to be the best accounting guy in the college, his help was immediately sought by those who were now in possession of the leaked-out question paper. They roused STJ from his sweet summer sleep around midnight and presented their case most earnestly.

Rubbing his eyes and feeling uneasy about the midnight intrusion and the desperate group huddled around him, STJ stared at the question paper for a while and concluded that it was not difficult at all. To the group, however, he pretended that the paper was too hard for him to solve. Obviously, STJ did not want to be associated with a criminal act that had the potential to discredit his good reputation and ruin his academic ambitions. At the same time, he was also aware that his refusal to solve the question paper for the group could have invited their ferocity and resulted in a needless commotion. But STJ was very lucky that day, for the group had no time to waste. The moment they heard STJ's no, they sprinted to the second-best accounting guy for help.

The next day, when STJ sat the exam, he was shocked to see the exact question paper that was leaked out the previous night. It was hard for him to understand how such a thing could ever happen in a college exam.

It wasn't just an isolated case of inefficiency on the part of the exam wing of the college, for the following night the same thing happened again; another question paper was leaked out, though this time STJ stayed away from it altogether. He just glanced at the paper to make sure that he knew the answers to the test questions.

But the greatest surprise erupted the morning after: the question paper handed out to the students this time was not the one that had been leaked out! It was a different question paper altogether! It shook everyone! While most of the students gazed at the question paper in utter disbelief, some yelled "No!" and "Not fair!" Some even felt the earth slip away from under their feet.

Inquiry revealed that someone, most probably a student whose conscience was not dead yet, had tipped off the exam wing about the leak; consequently, in the late hours of the night, the exam wing had replaced the original question paper with a new cyclostyled paper!

The exam wing had finally outwitted the students and defeated their plan. A few blockheaded students tried to boycott the paper by declaring it out of course, but their attempts failed, as most of the students did not buy their idea.

Terribly shaken by the two incidents, STJ and Khalid Hannan quietly moved to the New Campus Hostel on Canal Road to start the new year in more agreeable conditions.

Moving to the New Campus was no less eventful. The warden there had, of course, reserved a room for STJ and Hannan, but when the two got there, they discovered that the room was illegally occupied by a little-known student group from Kashmir called the KSG. The group had been told several times to vacate the room, but to no avail. As a last resort, the warden forcibly drove them out to house STJ and Hannan.

The very next day, as the two returned to their room after attending the day's lectures, they found the room occupied by KSG again. This time the group had gone a step further: they had thrown out the tenants' luggage rather rudely. "The *qabza* (occupation) group has once again made their presence felt!", remarked STJ.

The most logical thing to do in a situation like this was not to confront the illegal occupants but to see the warden at once, which the two did without wasting time. The warden, already a busy fellow, agreed to give the two a different room. At the same time, he made sure that the KSG guys were evicted and shown the door before dusk that day. And he padlocked the room thereafter.

The New Campus hostel was in many ways better than the old. It stood firmly in the vicinity of a serene lake, away from the deafening madness of the city center. It provided a tranquil learning environment, something that was terribly missing in the old building. "On the whole," recalls STJ, "it was great fun living together, particularly in the capacity of room incharge. Everybody in my room was under my control, and I made all decisions that my roommates had to follow. It was one compelling reason for me to stay in Lahore."

The Brothers' Fun Trip to Karachi

In April 1975, SAJ and STJ boarded the Karachi-bound express train in Lahore to see SKJ, who was residing in the Jinnah Courts Muslim Hostel (JCMH) of S.M. Commerce College. SKJ was there for his B.Com degree.

What facilitated such a financially challenging trip was the stipend of Rs. 1,400 that STJ had earned for securing third position in the diploma exam of the Punjab Technical Board. In those days, it was considered a huge amount of money—good enough to meet STJ's hostel expenses for at least seven months. Encouraged by this sudden acquisition of wealth and the confidence that comes with it, STJ had felt the need to share his unprecedented joy with SAJ, and together they had decided to make the best use of the money by visiting Karachi that year instead of the parental abode in Rawalpindi. They would enjoy their spring holidays in the company of SKJ, their more extroverted brother.

SAJ and STJ filled out the railway concession forms and got them signed by their respective institutions. In view of their new affluent status, the two booked the seats in the second class of the Awam Express, which was a clear departure from their third-class bookings of the past.

No journey begins without preparations, particularly when the trippers have money to spend. The two brothers visited Anarkali Bazaar, the busiest commercial center in Lahore, and purchased a pair of felt hats, sunglasses, and tee shirts. They were so excited about the forthcoming trip and the preparatory arrangements that without waiting for the journey to commence, they took out their purchases and put them on then and there, although the afternoon sun had already cooled down and the fading light of the evening had started to blur the images.

Taking advantage of the failing light, someone, perhaps a hostel resident who knew SAJ, drove his motorcycle dangerously close to the brothers and in a jiffy pulled SAJ's brand-new hat off his head before vanishing in the prevailing darkness. For a second, SAJ could not figure out what had happened. When he realized that his felt hat was missing, he did a quick calculation and discovered that it wasn't a huge loss—just seven rupees. With a lot of money still to be spent, the two hurried back to Anarkali and bought another hat. The thief could not undermine their resolve!

The next morning, the brothers dressed themselves up in pants and shirts, put on their felt hats and sunglasses, and boarded the Awam Express in the second class. Their uncharacteristic mannerisms made them conspicuous in the teeming crowd of travellers outside the Lahore railway station. It was, without doubt, a whole new experience for the brothers, who had never travelled in the second class before. The comfort of this new class was a pleasant surprise they would later share with SKJ.

It was all going well until STJ realized that he alone had been spending the money of his stipend thus far, and that SAJ had skilfully kept his own money intact. So, when dinner time came, STJ gathered courage and politely asked SAJ to buy the next meal for them. SAJ bluntly rejected such a possibility, saying that his pocket was as empty as an overturned bucket. He also told STJ that he had been under the impression that the entire cost of the trip would be borne by STJ alone, out of his stipend.

SAJ's response obviously disappointed STJ, but it didn't stop the latter from testing his brother's patience. Despite SAJ's refusal to pay for the food, STJ still believed that the growing hunger would sooner or later prompt his elder brother to change his mind. It didn't. Consequently, the two dragged their empty bellies on until midnight, about which time the train halted at Multan station and the passengers got off to straighten their legs and stretch their arms and buy snacks and drinks. The brothers also stepped out, though without knowing how to deal with their unbearable hunger.

A few minutes later, STJ noticed that his elder brother was missing. It worried him a little. He quickly did a 360-degree search and spotted SAJ standing beside a station vendor. "What is he doing there?" he asked himself. As he approached, he noticed that SAJ, who had earlier declared himself penniless, was now hastily eating a pack of *khoya*, a delicious cheese-like substance.

Caught in the act, SAJ appeared a little embarrassed. When STJ questioned him about his covert operation, SAJ justified it by saying that he had luckily found a fifty-paisa coin in his pocket, which he used to lessen his agonizing hunger. STJ had no choice but to believe his elder brother. Although STJ too badly needed to eat something very soon, it was no longer possible, for the wheels of the train were back in motion again.

The next day, the train finally arrived at the Karachi station. The brothers—exhausted, soiled, and starving—got off the train, only to be greeted by a blazing sun and a clear blue sky. Desperate to run away from the sizzling heat, they decided to take a bath right at the station. A quick survey of the site helped them locate a public tube-well. To it they ran, and without taking off any of the things they were wearing (tee shirts, felt hats, sunglasses), they sat down under the tap cross-legged and let the water slide down their soiled bodies for a good fifteen minutes.

The cold bath did refresh things a bit for the brothers, but it did nothing to mitigate their hunger. The next thing the brothers did was buy a dozen bananas! It wasn't a lot of money, just a couple of rupees. Since the two hadn't had anything to eat for days, they peeled the bananas one by one and consumed the whole purchase in a few minutes. The bananas gave them enough energy to walk to the bus stop and board a bus that would take them to JCMH.

On the way, the brothers busied themselves in a pleasant exchange that centered on their own extraordinary looks and mannerisms. "This tee shirt and these sunglasses make you look like the wealthiest and the healthiest man in the street," remarked SAJ. Conscious of his skinny structure, STJ enjoyed the comment very much and swelled a bit with pride. In fact, STJ realized that SAJ was quite right, as most of the pedestrians in the street appeared to have been what he called "severely struck by starvation."

After about an hour, the brothers were right at the gate of JCMH, and the guard on duty directed them to SKJ's room. The moment they entered the room, a tall guy carrying a mass of dense hair on his head greeted them. "Oh, you're here!" Then the towering man embraced them at the speed of lightning. The two brothers were obviously confused, because they had never known SKJ to be so tall and hairy and keen. While they were trying to solve the puzzle, SKJ walked into the room with a broad smile on his face.

Like a good host, SKJ at once escorted his brothers to the cafeteria for tea and snacks. There he disclosed that the tall guy who had greeted them in his room was his roommate Chaudhry. SKJ also revealed that at the hostel, "for obvious reasons," he had to conceal his Urdu-speaking identity and portray himself as a Punjabi-speaking student from Rawalpindi. It was a disclosure that shocked SAJ and STJ. Soon, however, they realized that SKJ was right in doing so, for they knew that people hailing from East Pakistan were generally looked on with suspicion, if not contempt. In view of this, SAJ and STJ were also now expected to hide not only SKJ's identity but also their own. This, according to SKJ, was necessary to prevent any awkward situation at JCMH.

In the evening, SKJ and Chaudhry accompanied the visitors on a general round of Karachi. Together they roamed the city, walking and riding buses and commenting on passersby and advertising boards and whatever their eyes could spot and stare at. Then fatigue got the better of their strength and pace, forcing them to take breaks. Breaks meant that they could enjoy the creamy *Farzand Ki Kulfi*, yummy ice cream, spicy *samosas*, and other roadside delicacies.

To entertain Chaudhry, SAJ also sang an old Punjabi song, at least he tried his best, though SKJ did not like the idea at all. SKJ had a valid reason to object: since SAJ knew very little Punjabi, his inability to sing the song properly could have exposed the true identities of the brothers, and that could have meant trouble for them. Full marks to SKJ, for he was able to avert an embarrassing situation by lying to Chaudhry that SAJ had forgotten much of his Punjabi because of his frequent interaction with his Urdu-speaking friends.

The brothers spent the next few days meeting relatives, which included uncles, aunties, cousins, and their children. These meetings were very useful and enlightening; at the same time, they provided the brothers with the much-awaited eating opportunities.

The brothers also visited the best cloth market in Karachi and bought a few pieces for trousers and shirts. Then they walked straight to the best tailor in the city and handed him the pieces for stitching, for they still had enough money to afford it.

Next, they headed toward the scenic beaches at Clifton, Hawks Bay, and Sands Pit. The fascinating rocky formation at Sands Pit in particular caught the brothers' attention, and they viewed this wonder of nature with awe and admiration. They also strolled to the nearby Manora Island, another popular picnic spot known for its towering lighthouse, and spent some time there enjoying the sights and sounds of nature and the aroma and freshness of a splendid warm day.

Even the most memorable of visits comes to an end, and this one was no exception. Two weeks of endless entertainment finally drew to a close. The brothers couldn't believe that half a month of joy had elapsed in such great haste.

Uncle Ziauddin's Amusing Tales

Uncle Ziauddin, our undisputed family benefactor, was a natural storyteller who narrated his tales in such a manner that they always sounded true and real. Clarity was the hallmark of his style, and together with his overflowing zeal, it produced a mesmerizing effect on the listeners. Most importantly, he enjoyed telling stories to people who valued his company more than his tales. SAJ and STJ, during their stay in Lahore, treasured both his company and his stories.

Most of Uncle Ziauddin's stories were very funny. One that SAJ and STJ still remember is titled "The Buffalo and the Woman in Veil." The brothers didn't believe it to be true for a number of years, though Uncle Ziauddin had made it sound like a real occurrence, something one expects from a master storyteller. It was several years after the telling of the story that the brothers discovered that the tale was indeed true; Uncle Ziauddin had smartly used fake names to hide real-life characters, in a way no listener could ever perceive. Here's the story.

Uncle Ziauddin had a friend by the name of Khudabaksh. He was a short fellow perpetually dressed in pajamas, a long shirt, and a weskit, besides a Kurakuli headgear and open shoes. And he had a typically Chinese beard.

Khudabaksh was known for doing unusual things, like climbing trees and resting on their branches for hours, or standing motionless on pavements as if lost, like a saint in contemplation. No one really understood why an ordinary mortal like him did those weird things.

Inquiry revealed that Khudabaksh routinely passed through a street where he would always encounter a herd of buffalos heading toward their destination. It was a sight Khudabaksh hated the most, one that made him utterly sick. The nauseating smell of the livestock would nearly suffocate him to death. "O God, help me get out of this. I can't take it anymore," he would plead almost every day. Soon Khudabaksh got fed up with his daily encounters with the smelly beasts and seriously began to ponder a way out.

After a day or two of contemplation, Khudabaksh figured out that the encounters were taking place largely due to his eye contact with the buffalos. He thought that he could easily avoid these encounters by lowering his gaze while walking through the street and assuming that the buffalos didn't really exist. Simple as that!

The next morning, when Khudabaksh tried his self-made solution, a terrible thing happened: he bumped into what he thought was a buffalo! A buffalo it was not. It was an ordinary woman in a black, head-to-toe burka. Thinking that he had collided with a buffalo, Khudabaksh yelled at full volume, "*Saalay Khuli Chorr Datay Hain.*" (Why do people let them loose?)

 # Early Childhood, the War, 20-A/1

THE NINTH CHILD OF MY PARENTS, I was born on January 15, 1968, in Dhaka, formerly a town of East Pakistan, today the capital of Bangladesh. I was only three when my family migrated to West Pakistan in view of the worsening crisis in the east wing; therefore, it's difficult for me to recall the ins and outs of the place of my birth or any event associated with it.

The 1971 war perpetrated by India was still raging when we settled in Satellite Town, Rawalpindi, in a large government rented house (20-A/1). Of the war, I can recall just a little. One incident, however, never quits my memory—Father holding his hunter's gun and aiming at a stray Indian jet that had infiltrated into a residential area in Rawalpindi. There was no way Father could have brought down the jet with that ordinary rifle of his. Perhaps it was his own little way of contributing to the cause of the Motherland, whose security was threatened by an unprovoked enemy. Later that day, as we huddled together to listen to the war update on the radio, we learned, to our great satisfaction, that the jet Father was trying to shoot down was in fact downed by an anti-aircraft gun of the Pakistan Army.

My memory of the 1971 war is limited to sirens and blackouts. A siren prompted us to turn off the lights and scurry to a safer place. Bathrooms, with their so-called double roof protection, were believed to be the safest place in the event of an air attack. Corners of ordinary rooms were also considered relatively secure. Another wartime safety measure involved coating the windowpanes with khaki paper or old newspapers to hoodwink the enemy.

Our 20-A/1 dwelling in Satellite Town was fairly large, with wide-open spaces in front and in back. A broad, extended walkway led to an old-fashioned garage stuffed with unwanted items. The graveled verandah (*usaraa*) at the rear served as a meeting place for occasional family get-togethers in the summer. The bedrooms were smaller in size, though greater in number—four or five at least. The kitchen stood at some distance from the rest of the house; after sunset, it would be a scary job to walk to the kitchen alone. The fear of getting devoured halfway by a nocturnal ghost often freaked me out. The same dreadful thought recurred in my dreams and often ended with a soundless midnight shriek.

We usually ate our meals in the dining room and occasionally in the kitchen. Eating in the kitchen was doubly delicious: the luxury of soft, inflating *roti* and sizzling *tarkaari*, all munched beside the kitchen stove in the coziest of settings.

The *tarkaaris*, or dishes, that our eyes and tongues got used to willingly or unwillingly over the years consisted of the following: *daal bhaat* (a soup of lentils and boiled rice), *aloo ke bhujia* (potato slices cooked in oil), *khichreeh aur aloo ka bherta* (a thick soup of rice and lentils eaten with mashed potatoes made whenever a family member had an aching stomach); *toree* (ridge gourd; Father used to pronounce it *torai*); *daal chana* (gram lentil) with *toree; kuddoo* (bottle gourd), and *karam kalla* (cabbage).

I can claim, without any fear of contradicting myself, that if any one vegetable could be credited with paying the most visits to our bellies, it would surely be *aloo* (potato). The second most frequent visitor would be *torai*. The least frequent visitors, for obvious reasons, would be chicken, meat, and fish, though the frequency of their visits did increase as the years rolled on. Also, the rice that we mostly ate, at least once a day, would be the yellow *joshi* type or the broken but tasty *khuddi* variety. These were gradually replaced by the sweet-scented whole basmati. Very rarely, the plain white rice when boiled assumed a sticky form called *gulhat*; it was consumed without enthusiasm.

Appended to the kitchen was a long, narrow, corridor-like

storeroom, where groceries and rarely used utensils were stocked. But, believe it or not, once this storeroom had been used as an intensive care unit for one of our domesticated goats that had fallen sick. Despite our best efforts, the poor ruminant could not be saved. A last agonizing shriek was all some of us heard one cold December midnight, which meant that it was all over for that hapless creature. The next morning, a sweeper (*mehtar*) was called to remove the carcass. Some non-Muslim sweepers presumably didn't mind eating the meat of dead animals.

A two-bedroom annex stood by the rear boundary wall of our 20-A/1 dwelling. It was inhabited by Akhtar *mamoon* (our maternal uncle), his wife (*mumaani*), their four sons, and their two daughters (our cousins). Father always referred to Akhtar *mamoon* as "Guard Sahib" because of his past career in the railways. There was an element of awe in Akhtar *mamoon's* personality, which earned him a lot of respect and veneration. Because of that, our contacts with him were few and far between. *Mumaani*, on the other hand, personified confidence; Mother always found solace and comfort in her presence. In fact, whenever Mother felt depressed or dejected, she sought *Mumaani's* company for support and strength. Almost every day, we mingled with our cousins and gossiped and played carom board and ludo together. It seldom occurred to us that they were a separate family unit.

At 20-A/1 we had a few varieties of fruit trees: mango, apricot, papaya, and lemon. The mangoes never lived to a ripe old age. They were plucked green and used to make the traditional mango pickle, *aam ka achaar*. It was not a simple process. The green mangoes were washed, cut into four or more pieces, freed of the pits (*ghutlee*), and laid out in the sunshine on a piece of cloth until they were dried out and softened. Then the pieces were put in a big earthen jar, the *boyaam*. Next, several kinds of spices, seeds, powders, and *karhwah tael* (mustard oil) were added. The jar was then kept in the sun for a week or so, during which time it was shaken once in a while to get the right mix of spices and flavor.

One *boyaam* of *achaar* would suffice for a whole year. Mother almost single-handedly carried out the entire work.

Unripe mangoes were also used to make the extremely appetizing *kutchla*—thinly sliced mango pulp mixed with *karhwah tael*, salt, and a kind of black seeds. It was best consumed with *daal bhaat*. *Aam ka achaar* and *kutchla* constituted a major, if not the only, spicy element in our lives!

Now a word about our meals. Our breakfast on weekdays by and large consisted of *Aloo ke bhujia, roti,* and omelet; on Sundays an additional item, like *firnee* (rice pudding), complemented it. Occasionally, instead of the plain *roti*, we would savor *aloo ka paratha* (chapati filled with boiled potato and fried lightly), or *daal ka paratha* (chapati filled with boiled gram lentil and fried lightly), or *chaukore* (square) *roti* softened with ghee or butter and eaten with fried eggs. Later additions to the morning menu included extra-dark *gajar ka halwa* (carrot halwa), honey, and orange marmalade.

Our lunch primarily consisted of *daal-bhaat* and a vegetable dish. Meat, for economic reasons, would be an occasional delicacy. Father could afford a kilo or two of meat once a week, with a piece or two flooded in curry for each family member.

For a number of years, we didn't use spoons to eat rice; instead, we used our right hand, the fingers in particular, disregarding the fact that some people considered the practice too primitive. We never felt any shame in doing what our parents did or what their parents did. Nonetheless, we were still free to use spoons if and when we wanted to use them. As the years rolled on, we began to use spoons more frequently, and the great tradition of eating food with bare hands gradually faded away.

20-A/1 Supplies

Throughout our stay at 20-A/1, SNJ and I, occasionally accompanied by Father, continued to fetch our monthly groceries from a shop at the bustling Commercial Market, a mile or so from where we lived. A white-bearded *maulvi* sahib, whose kindness as a seller was acknowledged by all, ran the shop. He was kind enough to accept deferred payments and was not irritated by occasional delays. Every now and then, he would serve us with a handful of raisins (*kishmish*) in exchange for used paper bags that we returned—a remarkable manifestation of his cheerful self.

Sometimes *maulvi* sahib exhibited his sense of humor too. Once, he told us how one letter or character could change sweetness into bitterness: "If you insert the Urdu letter *kaaf* between the letters *meem* and *sheen* of the word *kishmish*, it becomes *kashmakash*, which isn't as sweet as *kishmish;* instead, it is quite the opposite of what *kishmish* stands for." SNJ and I thoroughly enjoyed his witty remarks.

Supplies to be fetched were invariably decided by Mother in consultation with Father, though it was Father who would, after a thorough scrutiny, approve the list. Once the list was approved, it was our job to walk all the way to *maulvi* sahib's shop to get the supplies. Usually we carried two cotton bags (*thelay*) and a three-liter mustard oil canister. Mother stitched the bags at home from spare pieces of cloth reluctantly returned by tailors or from worn-out trousers and sofa covers. The aluminum oil canister had been with us for two decades or so before we stopped using it and started buying sealed oil cans in the 1980s.

It was fun carrying the empty bags and the canister, but once these were filled to capacity, it became a tedious task, often leading to quarrels, with both of us wanting to carry the lighter bag. Being the junior partner, I would always settle for the heavier bag, reluctantly of course. During one of the errands, I actually abandoned my bulky bag halfway to register my protest. SNJ, who realized what I'd done quite late, had to walk all the way back to retrieve it. When the two of us got home, SNJ raised hell and made a big issue of it.

Another task we performed jointly, at least once a month, was fetching flour and sugar from the local ration depot, a twenty-minute walk from our dwelling in Rawalpindi. Being the younger brother, I always had to carry the heavier flour bag that weighed, as far as I remember, twenty kilograms. Once in a while, however, SNJ let me hold the lighter sugar bag, which was half the weight of the flour bag, while he carried the flour bag. This he would do, I presume, to save me from running out of patience.

Without question, the rationing system, launched globally as early as the start of World War I, was not a constraint but a privilege enjoyed by many, including the government servants. In Pakistan, it was reintroduced after a gap of several years. However, to the great dismay of the beneficiaries, the government hastily abolished the system in April 1987, and it was never started again. The era of low-cost buying was over.

As for basic school supplies—lined sheets, fountain pens, pencils, erasers, and ink—Father purchased them at Javed Book Depot (or was it Rahman Book Depot?), a rather busy shop at the vibrant Commercial Market in Rawalpindi. The shop would get busier at the start of the new academic year when back-to-school shopping was at its peak. The owner of the shop was a compassionate gentleman who almost always heeded Father's discount petitions. In fact, with Father bargaining, there was no way a shopkeeper or a vendor could make more money than what he genuinely deserved. Father always preached and practiced bargaining as a tenet of the Sunnah of Prophet Muhammad (peace and blessings of Allah be upon him).

My Formal Schooling

My formal schooling began at Jinnah Preparatory School (JPS), Satellite Town, Rawalpindi, where I was admitted to kindergarten when I was four. Situated at a walking distance from our 20-A/1 residence, the school was known for its high standard of education as well as a relentless set of principles that parents and pupils were required to follow in letter and spirit. The principal, Dr. Abdul Haye Sheikh, a retired soldier, was a strict disciplinarian. He always wore a Jinnah cap to express his affection for the Founder of the Nation, Quaid-i-Azam Muhammad Ali Jinnah.

Most of the schoolteachers at JPS were strict and unforgiving and did not tolerate any breach of discipline. An academic lapse or failure on the part of a pupil always led to mental as well as physical punishment. For instance, I still remember being hit with a ruler by our math teacher; his favorite spot was the back of a student's hand. Obviously, it hurt a lot. My crime was that I had not done my homework.

JPS was a private school with an exorbitant tuition fee my father couldn't afford for long. For that very reason, as soon as I was promoted to Class 1, Father had me transferred to a less expensive Central Government Model School (CGMS), Rawalpindi, which was later renamed as Federal Government Model School (FGMS), Islamabad. My transfer to CGMS was also driven by the fact that my elder brother SNJ and sister Talat had been enrolled there since Class 1, so my admission to the same institution suited Father in that he could now apply for fee concessions.

FGMS was a coeducational school with just about equal male and female enrollment. It enjoyed a reasonably good reputation for quality education. Moreover, games like basketball, football (soccer), cricket, and table tennis were regularly played in the school playground and indoor courts to promote healthy competition between different classes. In addition, contests were held among different groups of students called "houses" named after the leading freedom fighters of the country: Jinnah, Iqbal, Liaqat, Sir Syed, Jauhar, etc. Such activities generated a lot of interest for students and provided them great relief from the droning drill of academic pursuits.

At FGMS I remained a mediocre student, though I never stooped below average. Also, despite being an incorrigible introvert, I did make a few friends, some of whom still get in touch with me once in a blue moon.

One always learns from schoolteachers, be they callous or caring. Some occupy our thoughts more favorably than others. I was fortunate to have quite a fascinating variety of teachers. I still remember the soft-spoken Sir Naqvi, who taught us elementary science and much more; the ferocious Sir Iqbal, who gave us lessons in social studies; the frank Sir Shaukat, our drawing teacher, who was equally popular among boys and girls; the impulsive Sir Ikraam, the left-handed physical training instructor and supervisor of games, who always wore a Chinese cap to hide his baldness.

While most teachers dictated from readymade notes, there were a few, like Sir Naqvi, who would go beyond the frontiers of the curriculum to share their own ideas and life experiences. That added some sense to the otherwise tedious learning process; above all, it encouraged the class to come up with fascinating queries leading to lively discussions.

Being a less bookish student with a poor capacity for memorizing notes, I would study an extra hour or so at home every day to keep pace with classmates. Father, who knew our shortcomings more than anybody else, would keep pressing us for hard work: "Work hard or else you will end up selling *chena badaam* (peanuts)."

I never had any difficulty with English, social studies, Islamiyat, and general science, but mathematics was a hard nut to crack—and it still is. Thank God, I had no further interaction with math once I passed my secondary school examination in 1982.

The purely religious part of our education was looked after by a *qari* sahib, who visited our house almost every day through our elementary school years until we completed our preliminary reading of the Holy Quran. He would teach us the basics of recitation, pronunciation in particular, and make us memorize smaller verses. SNJ, Tahir, and I would sit cross-legged in front of *qari* sahib and repeat the words and verses after him. The *qari* sahib would gently pat us with his stick whenever our concentration lapsed or we failed to do our homework.

Coexisting with Hens

If memory serves me right, domesticated hens continued to coexist with us until 1981, the year we moved to Islamabad. We had quite a few, ranging from the *sufaid* (white), the *laal* (red), and the *kaali* (black) types to the tougher *chitkabri* (spotted) variety. The *chitkabri*, I presume, had the longest association with us, and consequently her departure saddened us the most. Slaughtering her was one of the toughest decisions Father had to make in the face of his strong personal opposition to the idea. Of course we also didn't like it, but moving to a posh sector in Islamabad, the capital city, demanded a visible change in lifestyle and attitudes. Keeping hens or any other animals in the capital city was considered crude and primitive. Whatever the reason or pretext, the loss of *chitkabri* was devastating, considering she had served us for so many years. Her departure haunted us for days. A pressure cooker, not an ordinary *degchi*, was what softened her!

There was a time when SAJ, SKJ, and STJ each had a self-proclaimed *murghee* (hen) of his own—the *sufaid*, the *laal,* and the *kaali* respectively. As per a verbal agreement, the egg laid by the *sufaid* belonged to SAJ; the one laid by the *laal* belonged to SKJ; and STJ had the right to the egg laid by the *kaali*. A post egg-laying call by a hen would alert the three. Without delay, they would all run to the hen's coop, but only the rightful owner of the egg-laying hen could grab her egg. The other two would wait for their hens to lay eggs. In any case, the egg was seized as soon as it was laid.

The agreement among the brothers remained in effect for a few years before it was broken to make the whole egg business a little more competitive. It only led to egg-snatching incidents, claims, and counterclaims.

There were two ways in which the egg was eaten—*khara anda* (fried with the yolk intact) or *piaz wala anda* (omelet). Sometimes the egg would be fried, cut into square pieces, and the pieces added to a separately made curry. Rarely did we eat it boiled. A boiled egg was better known as *usna hua anda*.

The 20-A/1 residence with its large open area in front and in back provided ample space for hens to move about freely, hunt small insects and worms, and lay eggs at will. Occasionally, a hen would be made to sit on a dozen or so eggs to get a fresh crop of chicks. Normally they would hatch in three to four weeks. Once out of their shells, the chicks would be meticulously guarded against greedy cats and low-flying eagles. Since twenty-four-hour surveillance was not possible, many chicks were easily attacked and snatched by probing predators. Only a few lucky ones survived to grow into useful hens.

Although some family members would never agree with the idea of domesticating hens, Father almost religiously believed in the usefulness of such a notion. Anyone who tried to argue against it often met his stiff resistance, which sometimes bordered on rebuke: "No one dare tell me what is right and what is wrong." STJ in particular was bitterly opposed to the keeping of hens, which he demonstrated once by selling off all the hens to a vendor at throwaway prices. He was able to do so because Father was not around. When Father returned home and was briefed about the transaction, he reacted with a lot of sound and fury.

For economical reasons, I presume, Father bought live hens at the meat shop and slaughtered them at home. That meant a lot of work for Mother, for she was required to boil and strip and clean and chop the slaughtered chicken, a distressing duty indeed. Surprisingly, Mother never complained about it. That was not all—it was also Mother's job to clean the floor at least two times a day to purge it of hen droppings, or *laahi*.

A hen that fell sick would be given *lehsun* (garlic bits), which was thought to make her better again. It was more of a superstitious belief than a fact of science. And a hen that reached the end of her egg-laying career was dismissed as a *kuruk murghee* and slaughtered.

Father slaughtered the hen according to the Muslim law.

That principally includes aligning the head of the hen with the Qibla, the Kaaba in Makkah, and reciting Allah-o-Akbar (Allah is Great) while cutting the main blood vessels around the throat and the wind pipe, but leaving the spinal cord intact. This way all the blood in the vessels spills out. An ordinary kitchen knife is used, but a very sharp one, so that the animal suffers the least.

This reminds me of an interesting incident. Once Father was in the middle of a hen slaughtering session when he realized, rather late, that the knife he was using wasn't doing the job. In desperation, he commanded us to fetch a sharper knife at once. But no other knife was readily available. Frustrated, he directed us in a thunderous voice to bring a shaving blade, which we did at once, and so the poor creature was relieved of her ordeal.

Once we had a hostile rooster whose multicolored plumage gave him a royal appearance. He was adamantly punctual with his wake-up calls early in the morning. We continued to heed his calls until a distant relative of ours arrived one fine morning with a death sentence for the hapless creature. It wasn't easy to silence the lively bird; like the *chitkabri*, it took a few hours to soften into an edible form.

Goryeya Hunting

With quite a few egg-laying hens in our possession and a couple of roosters to guard them, we shouldn't have felt the need for further amusement. But we invented a rather bizarre way of entertaining ourselves anyway: hunting sparrows (*goryeya*).

While my elder brothers might have their own reasons, I couldn't understand why on earth it was necessary to trap and kill such tiny and harmless creatures as sparrows, for we weren't faced with famine, nor were the birds destroying our cash crops. What was it then? Was it the untamed human instinct that overshadows reason and promotes excitement?

Sparrows frequently visited the large concrete backyard of our 20-A/1 residence in search of leftover grains and seeds. They came in large numbers, particularly in the summer. The idea to hunt them for food was never discussed or debated at home, and I for sure didn't know who had first started it.

There were two steps to the hunting process. First, a fistful of rice grains were scattered over a specified area of the backyard in full view of the local birds. Second, right in the center of this area, a big bamboo basket (*tokra*) was laid upside down with a portion of it raised a foot or so from the ground using a vertical stick tied to a string. One of us held the other end of the string in our hiding place while waiting for the sparrows to land. The hungry sparrows would sooner or later land in the food area and start picking up the grains oblivious to the danger that lay ahead. As soon as some of them entered the danger zone—the area under the inverted basket—the string would be pulled, thus trapping the sparrows inside the basket.

The trapped sparrows were then transferred to the net-equipped kitchen window that served as a temporary cage for the doomed birds. They were taken out of the cage one by one and slaughtered with a razor blade. Next, it would be Mother's job to strip the birds, remove the unwanted parts, and cook the meat the way she would cook chicken. The final dish, however, tasted a lot better than chicken. But Mother, I am pretty sure, didn't really appreciate all that, and she soon got fed up with it. As a result, we had to forego the controversial pursuit once and for all.

Saifull

He was our next-door neighbor at 20-A/1, a middle-aged, heavyweight champion of nothingness. His first name was Saifull, and we never cared what his full name was. Nor had we any idea where he worked, or what he did for a living. Probably he was a government servant of some sort. One thing we knew for sure was that he loved eating, which was evident from his fleshy face and bulging belly. In the summer we would sometimes see him in half pants and tee shirt.

For unknown reasons, we were far short of being ideal neighbors. I cannot recall our family ever visiting the Saifulls or one of them knocking at our door even once in the six-plus years of our neighborly existence. Apparently, we were not on the same wavelength.

One occurrence of which Saifull was the villain refuses to quit my memory. It all happened on a pleasant summer day in 1978. SNJ and I were standing on the roof of the 20-A/1 part of the duplex trying our hand at kite flying. Although we were taking great care not to cross over to Saifull's part of the common roof, the pounding caused by our feet constantly moving back and forth unfortunately awakened Saifull from his sweet summer sleep. Obviously, the poor fellow was enraged. His reaction was swift and stern: he came running through his bedroom onto our portion of the roof, ready to smack us as hard as he could. Sensing danger, SNJ fled the scene at once, leaving me at the mercy of a provoked Saifull. He was about to slap me with his beefy hand when he caught sight of Father entering the house through the main gate. In fact, Father had seen Saifull's hostile posture and was now looking straight into his neighbor's eyes. I could clearly see rage building up on Father's face. His message was loud and clear. Saifull had no option but to leave me unharmed. That was not all—Father was so infuriated by Saifull's raising of hand against me that without putting it off for another day, he walked up to him and in very clear terms rebuked him for intimidating me: "Don't you dare!" That was enough to bring the robust neighbor to his senses.

Another event that involved Saifull as the key character had to do with a certain apricot tree that stood right on the imaginary line dividing the two portions of the 20-A duplex. The tree carried a rich load of apricots in the right season, and we all plucked the fruit at will and never tired of relishing its delectable taste. Although we had no objection to the plucking of the fruit by Saifull and his family, since they too had the right to it, Saifull would always maintain that the whole tree belonged to him and that he alone had the right to pluck its fruit.

It hadn't been much of a dispute in the early days of our coexistence; however, as days rolled on, Saifull became increasingly upset about not getting a hundred percent of the yield. He was violently vocal about the issue, so much so that it became an everyday quarrel. Father, who would normally have a huge reserve of patience, didn't really care about the issue at first, but when Saifull remained adamant on his unlawful claim, in a frustratingly vicious way, Father literally lifted his hands toward the heavens and prayed to Allah to make the tree fruitless! It was quite an unusual prayer, a prayer no one would have ever associated with Father. Father must have thought that it was the only way to settle the dispute once and for all.

And, believe it or not, it did settle the issue forever. Father's prayers were answered the very next year, for the disputed tree never bore fruit again!

No family member, except Uncle Younus, father of Anas bhai, had any knowledge of this strange occurrence. Father had shared it with Uncle Younus when the latter visited us in Rawalpindi in December 1976. When STJ visited Karachi, a year or two later, Uncle Younus narrated the incredible tale of the apricot tree to him.

Our next-door neighbor on the left was a tall man in his forties who had recently migrated from East Punjab, India. One thing I can't forget about him is that he had a pair of stout buffalos that he kept in his backyard, which was quite an unusual sight in the neighborhood. It was not very bothersome to us, for the owner of the house would send us about a kilo or two of buffalo milk every day. Initially we thought that the fat-rich milk was given to us free of cost, but we discovered it later that it was actually sold to us. The milk was so thick and creamy that we could add water to it to make two kilos out of one. No buffalo, however chubby, could beat these buffalos in performance.

Wajid Sahib

One of Father's frequent visitors was Wajid sahib, who looked more like a retired army officer than an ordinary civilian like us. He had a brownish complexion, a wide forehead, and two big ears; and he had his hair, or what remained of his hair, neatly combed back, a style associated with the good old people of the seventies. The broadness of his face never escaped our attention. He rode a Sohrab bicycle to our 20-A/1 residence, which probably was the reason he was still fit at sixty.

Wajid sahib didn't drop by to sip tea or gobble up biscuits, although we almost always served him with snacks; he would come to seek Father's help in drafting official letters. Sometimes Father dictated notes to him in the drawing room, where we never ventured in their presence.

Wajid sahib probably worked as a senior clerk in the Ministry of Defence, where Father worked as a section officer. He always came with a bunch of files tied to the rear rack of his bicycle. He usually stayed for an hour or so. It was one to one; we never had any meaningful interaction with him, nor did he ever show any interest in us.

We continued to see Wajid sahib as long as we lived in Satellite Town, Rawalpindi. Then he stopped coming. We never asked Father why he had stopped coming. We never heard of him again.

 # The Turkish Delight

IN OCTOBER 1977, FATHER WAS SELECTED by the Ministry of Defence, where he worked as a section officer, for appointment as Assistant Secretary at the Combined Military Planning Staff (CMPS), Central Treaty Organization (CENTO), headquartered in Ankara, Turkey. Established in 1959 by Iran, Pakistan, Turkey, and the United Kingdom as a mutual defense and security organization, CENTO eventually took the form of an alliance against the interests of the Soviet Union. Although the United States was not an official member of CENTO, it covertly supported the objectives of the organization.

It was a three-year posting, with five members of the family allowed to accompany Father. Father chose Mother and the four younger children—Tahir, Shahina, Farhat, and me. Although the posting promised monetary benefits, besides a wealth of international experience, it required Father to leave more than half of his family behind. No wonder it was a difficult choice Father had to make. What eventually prompted him to go ahead with the trip was the immense confidence he had in the abilities of his elder sons and daughters. He knew that they would be able to cope with the challenges of life in his absence.

The six of us landed at Ankara Esenboga Airport on a nippy November morning in 1977 and were officially driven from the airport to a reasonably good hotel in the city center. That was to be our temporary lodging. Despite ideal conditions, well furnished rooms, and excellent food, I (and I believe the rest of the family too) had great difficulty coming to terms with the alien setting and often dreamed of returning home at the earliest opportunity.

Father was the first to get used to the new surroundings, and he reported for duty at CENTO on the eighth of that month.

After staying at the Keykan Hotel for a month or so, we moved to a three-room apartment in a prime residential district away from the hustle and bustle of downtown Ankara. The apartment stood at an unusually high altitude, much higher than that of the adjoining areas, which enabled us to view the tops of houses and apartments in the immediate area as well as the narrow zigzagging, inclining, and declining streets separating the dwellings.

It was here that we had our first physical contact with snow, which we had seen only on television or heard stories about. It greatly stirred up our imagination the first time we gazed at the soft, white flakes tumbling down from the frozen sky. How swiftly it romanticized the atmosphere! There were days when it snowed from dawn to dusk, shrouding the roads and streets and grass and trees and rooftops with a fluffy white sheet, the kind of which we had never seen before. The whole neighborhood, as far as we could see, would wake up dressed in white. While it pleased us all, it didn't augur well for the municipal guys, who now had the additional job of restoring traffic and business.

The Turkish people are very particular about health and hygiene, which is an integral part of their lives. First thing in the morning, a Turkish housewife would scrub the nooks and corners of her house, including the windowpanes, almost religiously, so that the house glittered like a gem.

Strong family relations, generosity, and hospitality are very much central to the Turkish way of living. Above all, the Turkish people's commitment to Muslim brotherhood is phenomenal. In particular, their love for Pakistan and its people is unparalleled. I witnessed this whenever I interacted with my Turkish friends and their families. I was always treated with amazing affection and care. I would always feel the invincible strength of brotherhood in those meetings.

Pakistan Embassy School

As soon as Father joined CENTO, his next immediate concern was to get the four of us admitted to a good school. The children of Pakistanis working at CENTO mostly studied at the Pakistan Embassy International Study Group (PEISG), located at a ten-minute drive from where we resided in Ankara. Primarily meant for Pakistani children, the school also accepted students from other nations. The medium of instruction was, of course, English. Farhat and I were admitted to Class 7, whereas Shahina and Tahir were both placed in Class 5.

The school principal, Mrs. Syed, a middle-aged Pakistani by origin, was a lady of gentle manners and strong managerial skills. During the rehearsal for the annual school function in 1978, she developed a special fondness for me because of what she called my natural ability to recite verses from the Holy Quran. I have never considered myself a good *qari* for the simple reason that I don't quite understand the Arabic language, though I have always enjoyed reciting the holy verses. No wonder I was a little surprised when Mrs. Syed picked me from the entire school enrollment to do the recitation at the start of the annual function.

My classroom at PEISG was a small global village of a sort inhabited by children from Pakistan, Iran, Turkey, Jordan, Yugoslavia, the United States, and some other countries. Karem Basul, a smart boy from Jordan, became my best friend at first sight and remained so throughout our stay in Ankara. Despite being an Arab, Basul's English accent was immaculate and his handwriting fabulous. We sat next to each other in class and often helped each other with class work. At the time of parting, we both vowed to remain in touch with each other through correspondence; however, the letter that I wrote to Basul soon after arriving in Pakistan probably got lost in the mail, for I never received his reply. I was a little disappointed that we couldn't keep up our communication after such a promising start.

It did not take me long to make friends with Turkish boys

of my age group. They primarily included a few who lived in the basement of the apartment building where we resided, while others lived in the adjoining areas. Almost all of them belonged to middle or lower-middle classes. They conversed and joked and played together. Soccer was their favorite pastime, and they played it with a cheap plastic ball about half the size of a soccer ball. I was a hesitant starter, though I soon mingled with the boys and became a regular member of their team.

These Turkish teenagers also played another game, a rather strange game, in which a three- or four-foot PVC pipe, slender and hollow, was used to shoot paper cones at passersby. The paper cone was inserted into the pipe and forced out with a strong blow from the mouth. These cheap missiles were launched from hideouts in and around the houses. I once came under a surprise attack as a barrage of little missiles hit me from all directions. I had no idea what was going on until a passerby told me that it was just a game played by kids. Of course none of the missiles was deadly!

More of Turkey, the Dream Pilgrimage

In 1978 our parents seized a golden opportunity to perform Hajj, thanks to a compassionate Pakistani settled in Ankara. It was his annual practice to drive to Makkah, via Syria and Jordan, along with a group of intending Hajjis who all shared the travel expenses with him.

Again it was a difficult decision our parents had to make, the decision to leave the four of us behind. However, Father's CENTO colleagues and neighborhood friends, including some Pakistani families, would visit us every now and then during our parents' absence for a month or so. Our next-door neighbor, a kind Turkish woman in her seventies who looked more European than Asian, also took good care of us and more than once sent us bowls of mouthwatering macaroni. Some Pakistani families in the neighborhood who frequently visited us included Imtiaz sahib, Ashraf sahib, Izhar, and Altaf.

Although the Turkish people living in the vicinity were generally very cordial and friendly, the family living in the basement of the building in which we resided was immensely hospitable. Their two boys, both young teenagers (one was Yusef, the other's name I can't recall), instantly became my friends. At first, I was more inclined toward the younger of the two, the one who wore glasses, but with the passage of time my inclination shifted to his elder brother for reasons I still can't fathom. Probably he was more introverted than his younger brother. Probably he was late to reveal his true self. Probably there was a wavelength issue. Whatever the reason, there was very little to choose between the two; they both exhibited excellent manners and refined character. I was pretty sure that they hailed from a noble family. Frequent interaction with them and their family revealed that they were indeed spiritually advanced. Once, the boys' elder sister was so overwhelmed upon listening to a recitation of the Holy Quran by the legendary Qari Abdul Basit of Egypt that she ran upstairs to ask us about the Qari and the audio cassette of him reciting that we had been playing and she had overheard. Father had brought just one copy of the cassette from Saudi Arabia at the time of his pilgrimage to Makkah, and there was no way we could forgo the prized possession. However, we did lend them the cassette for a few weeks.

Living in the neighborhood was another boy, short and stout and red-faced: Mujtaba. He was the bread-seller's son and looked more mature than his age. He occasionally joined us for the evening soccer game. Once I was caught in a brief scuffle with him in the middle of a game. Unable to snatch the ball, Mujtaba had punched me in the face for no fault of mine. I retaliated with a kick in his ass. We were both red with rage when the basement boys intervened, disengaged us, and brought us to our senses. A few hours later, Mujtaba's mother visited us to apologize. I told her that it was only a petty incident that did not necessitate an apology, that I had no bitterness against Mujtaba, and that his beautiful name and friendship meant a lot to me.

We were in Ankara when we heard the news of hanging of Zulfiqar Ali Bhutto (ZAB), our former prime minister. He was sentenced to death for the murder of a political opponent following a trial in the Supreme Court of Pakistan that his followers dubbed flawed. Despite international appeals for clemency, he was sent to the gallows in a Rawalpindi jail on April 4, 1979. To many people in Turkey, it was a bolt from the blue. By and large, the Turkish people had a favorable image of ZAB as a leader of the Muslim world and greatly valued his endeavor for Muslim unity, though some thought that it was this image of his that had actually led to his undoing. Others maintained that he was more audacious than prudent. I was too young at the time to interpret politics or be part of a meaningful discussion on the subject.

Following the Islamic revolution in Iran in 1979, the new Iranian government announced its withdrawal from CENTO. Shortly afterward, Pakistan followed suit, arguing that Iran's withdrawal had rendered the organization useless. CENTO became defunct. As a result, all the military staffers were relieved of their duties on May 19, 1979, and the civil staffers were laid-off in October the same year.

Because of the abrupt dissolution of CENTO, our stay in Turkey was shortened to a little over two years. Obviously, we were not ready for a premature end to this pleasure trip, but there was nothing we could do. Before setting off for home, Father decided to go round Turkey's historical sites and attractions, something we all had been eagerly waiting for. It cheered us up.

The places we were fortunate to visit included the splendid Ataturk mausoleum (the Anitkabir) in Ankara, the majestic *masjids* (mosques), the Topkapi museum in Istanbul, and the grand tomb of Hazrat Maulana Jalaluddin Rumi, the great Sufi poet, in Konya.

The Anitkabir, which sits atop a hill overlooking the city, is guarded by a smartly dressed ceremonial contingent. We went inside the marbled structure to take a look at the great collection from Ataturk's life and work, as well as stamps, coins, and other valuable objects.

The grand *masjids* in Istanbul, many of which were built in the fifteenth century, are still in good shape and open to worship and visits by tourists from across the globe. They reflect the true Islamic color of modern Turkey. The Blue Mosque, Sultanahmet Camii, in particular captured our attention, and we all went inside to offer prayers. A caretaker told us that "it is the most famous mosque in Turkey, one of a kind, with its elegant six minarets."

Our visit to the Topkapi Palace Museum was one gem of an experience, a spiritual resurgence that brought us in direct contact with some of the rarest relics a Muslim could ever dream of seeing. Some are as holy as these: The Holy Prophet's bamboo bow, two of his swords, his letter in a gold case, soil from his grave, hair from his beard, his footprint, and some of his teeth. Peace and blessings of Allah be upon him.

In addition, we saw the very copy of the Holy Quran that Hazrat Usman (RA), the third caliph of Islam, had been reciting from when he was martyred by a foe. We could clearly see the dried drops of blood on the pages. It filled us with awe and respect.

The return trip was even more rewarding. Our first stopover was one of the most sacred places in the world: Madina Sharif. Upon arriving, we rented a room in a building facing the majestic Masjid-e-Nabvi. No wonder we were excited to enter one of the greatest places on earth, a place where Prophet Muhammad (upon whom be peace and blessings of Allah) had practiced and preached the last and final message of God to mankind. It is hard—almost impossible—to describe the extraordinary character of this great city. It is a unique experience, a one-of-a-kind spiritual odyssey that teaches the true meaning and purpose of life. It was here that we had the greatest honor of beholding the Roza-e-Mubarak, the shrine of Prophet Muhammad (upon whom be peace and blessings of Allah), the last and final messenger of God. Standing by the holiest of shrines, my mind meditated on his eternal message of truth, justice, peace, and all the other virtues upon which he modeled his own life for the entire humanity to emulate.

We stayed in Madina for nine days completing the traditional forty prayers, from May 20 to 27, 1979, in the blessed sanctuary of Masjid-e-Nabvi. The next day, we flew from Madina to Jeddah; and in Jeddah we took a taxi to Makkah. We rented a room in a hotel facing the Baitullah, Khana-e-Ka'abah. This holiest place on earth enjoys a unique status that makes it incomparable to any other place in the world. Over a billion Muslims from across the globe visit the place all year round, particularly during the Hajj pilgrimage. A resident of the city told us that during Hajj, Makkah stages the largest gathering of worshippers in the world.

Availing of the great opportunity, all of us wrapped ourselves in *ihram*, the plain white garment that pilgrims wear, and recited *talbiyah*, a short prayer chanted by the pilgrims, and performed Umrah and Tawaaf. Our parents also performed Umrah on behalf of their deceased parents. Father and I were fortunate enough to kiss the Hajar al-Aswad, the Black Stone. We also went around Maqam-e-Ibrahim, the spot where Prophet Ibrahim had stood for hours building the Ka'abah. We also quenched our thirst at the Well of Zamzam and filled some bottles with the holy water to take home.

No range of vocabulary can adequately describe the great spiritual experience one goes through in and around the Ka'abah!

Before leaving Makkah, we also visited Jannatul Baqi, where the great imams of Islam and the Prophet's near and dear ones are resting in eternal peace. We also stopped for a while at Masjid-e-Quba, Islam's first mosque, and also Masjid Qiblatayn, the mosque where Allah had commanded the Holy Prophet to change the Qiblah (prayer direction) from Masjid al-Aqsa (Jerusalem) to the Holy Ka'abah (Makkah). All of us offered prayers in each of these mosques before leaving for Jeddah, where we boarded a PIA plane for Pakistan.

 # Back Sweet Home, Father's Modesty

WE REACHED KARACHI ON THE FIRST of June 1979, a fairly hot summer day mellowed somewhat by a gentle breeze. Right away we took a cab to Uncle Zafir's house in Nazimabad No. II. He and his family were extremely delighted to receive us. It was the first time that I had a close look at Uncle Zafir after a gap of several years. To my pleasant surprise, I noticed that he had a striking resemblance to Father, except that his skin color was a shade darker. But they were both of the same height and wore glasses. Above all, Uncle Zafir too had a heart of gold. He entertained the six of us for eight days in his small house, which was ample proof of his generosity.

In Karachi, we also visited some of our other relatives, both close and distant, who lived in the neighborhood. We left for Rawalpindi on the morning of June 9, 1979, and after a two-hour peaceful flight, we were received at the Chaklala Airport by a lanky STJ carrying a dense growth of hair on his head and accompanied by a robust Ashfaq bhai, our cousin.

Indeed, home is where the heart is!

Each one of us heaved a sigh of relief and struggled to control our emotions as we reunited with the rest of the family. Hugs and handshakes and smiles and greetings followed. We spent the rest of the day—and the following week—talking about Turkey, the people we had interacted with, the places we had visited, and the good things that we had learned, besides a little English.

A few weeks before leaving Ankara for Rawalpindi, Father had ordered several household items from the Osterman catalogue (an American consumer products company), including a two-door refrigerator, a color television, a cassette player, a sewing machine, a cooking range, clocks, cutlery, and glassware. The shipment arrived in Rawalpindi a month or so after our return. As the big cargo truck was backing up through the wide gates of our residence, our faces lit up with excitement and expectations. Some of us even began to assume that the long spell of economic drought was finally over.

But none of us ever ignored our modest beginnings and the great value of the struggle that had fashioned our childhood and much of our youth. Father always led by example. For instance, he didn't let us throw away anything that could be put to use. This included the wooden Osterman container. Father hired a carpenter and had him chop and level the container wood into a dozen *chaukis* (bed frames) and a few small side tables.

Strictly adhering to his no-waste principle, Father would not let us trash any unused pieces of wood, pipes, wires, nails, screws, and stuff like that, despite our repeated objections to storing them at home. We were too naïve to appreciate his point in our youthful days, but we were able to do so when most of the things he had made us save were eventually used to our benefit. Such was his foresight!

Forgotten Promotion, Delegation to China

Father resumed his duties in the Ministry of Defence a month or so after returning from Turkey. During his absence, his case for seniority in service had already been decided; he had been elevated to BPS-18 with retroactive effect. In fact, Father had become eligible for the promotion a few years earlier, for prior to his transfer from the government of East Pakistan to the government of West Pakistan in 1971, he had not only passed the Departmental Examination held by the Public Service Commission, East Pakistan, but had also completed a two-month training at the Gazetted Officers Training Academy, Dacca, qualifying for promotion to the post of Deputy Secretary. It was in April 1979, however, that his name and names of two other section officers were sent to the governor of East Pakistan for the aforesaid promotion. Unfortunately, due to the worsening law-and-order situation in East Pakistan and the subsequent infiltration of the Indian Army, these officers' well-deserved promotions could not be communicated to the government of West Pakistan. Had Father been promoted as Deputy Secretary in April 1971, he would have been elevated to the post of joint secretary or even additional secretary in due course. Regrettably, no one at the top ever felt the need to set things right.

In April 1980, Father was selected to lead an official delegation to China for talks on erecting pillars marking the end of Pakistan's northern border at the Khunjerab Pass, the highest point on the Karakoram Highway. The delegation also included members of the GHQ, Survey of Pakistan, and the Magistrate of Hunza. The two sides met 50 kilometers inside the Chinese territory, exchanged greetings and gifts, and conversed for twelve hours before reaching a unanimous agreement on all issues. The agreement further strengthened the existing bonds of friendship between the two countries. It also gave Father a good reason to feel proud of his role in making the momentous agreement a reality.

In February 1982, Father was promoted to the rank of Deputy Secretary, BPS-19, and posted at the States and Frontier Regions Division (SAFRON), Pakistan Secretariat, Islamabad. On July 9, 1982, he reached the age of superannuation and was set to retire when, on the advice of the SAFRON Secretary, the Establishment Division reemployed Father for another two years. That period ended on July 9, 1984. And with that ended Father's forty-three years of active public service.

Back to School

Without doubt, Turkey did wonders for my confidence, broadened my mental horizons, and improved my English a bit. These were quite instrumental in my academic pursuits. Although I was a mediocre student when I rejoined F.G. Model School after a two-year break, I was still considered for a Class 8 scholarship exam. I did pass the exam but could not qualify for a stipend. It didn't matter in the least, because I wasn't expected to qualify for the stipend in the first place, given my past academic performance. What mattered more to me was that my two-year absence from the country had not cost me my school friends: none of them had broken ranks.

There was general contentment in the family in 1982 when SNJ and I passed the matriculation examination in the first division, though it didn't mean A grade; nor did it warranty a hoo-ha celebration or throwing a party. It only meant that the job was far from over and that we had to exert a lot more effort to get anywhere near a desirable performance.

As soon as we got our secondary school certificates, SNJ and I, like so many other graduates, were faced with two options: medicine or engineering. It wasn't easy for us to decide, so we took the matter to the highest family court—Father. He pondered for a while and then gave his verdict: I was to join premedicine, while SNJ was to try preengineering. Father argued that the family was in dire need of another doctor, besides Ashraf bhai, and a good engineer. Father's idea made a lot of sense, though we brothers weren't confident enough to make his dream come true.

Our next academic station was F.G. College for Men, H-8, Islamabad. The best thing about the college was not its reputation or standard of education, but its location. It stood away from the noisy and dusty traffic of Peshawar Morh. Moreover, it was in this college that I had my first contact with three main student groups referred to as "the union": the Islami Jamiat Talba (or simply Jamiat), the People's Students Federation (PSF), and the Muslim

Students Federation (MSF). These functioned as the youth wings of the three major political parties of the country: the Jamaat-e-Islami, the Pakistan People's Party, and the Pakistan Muslim League, respectively. Their activities, particularly on election days, symbolized much of the hustle and bustle of college life.

Of the three student groups, Jamiat demonstrated the greatest zeal and discipline. They were the first to welcome and greet us. However, we never took part in any union-related activity other than casting our vote on election days.

Variety is the Spice of Life: Teachers

As far as academic pursuits are concerned, I was fortunate to have teachers who knew their subjects well: Prof. Dr. Pervez of the physics department, Prof. Zaidi of the chemistry department, and Prof. Anwar Kazim of the English department, to name only a few.

Prof. Pervez had a wonderful notion of teaching, one that laid focus on the basics. It didn't matter to him, for instance, if he took a whole month or even more to explain the fundamental concepts before taking up the complicated ideas. No wonder he spent almost two months explaining scalars and vectors when we had our first interaction with college physics.

Prof. Sayedain Zaidi, who taught us inorganic chemistry, was quite the opposite. He was quick and vocal, and he wouldn't give us any time to relax. He used chalk a lot; it didn't bother him a bit if it whitened his black pants or the tip of his nose. One more thing: the constantly red interior of his mouth indicated that he was a habitual *paan*-eater. That did not matter in any way, for he was an excellent instructor.

We also had another professor by the same last name, Zaidi, though he was much shorter. He taught us organic chemistry, and what a brilliant brain he was! I never saw him open the textbook to look up something; his brain was the textbook. We always envied his depth of knowledge and the confidence with which he dictated foot-long formulas and equations without once opening the textbook. It was because of him that I became interested in organic chemistry and went on to score fifty out of fifty on the subject in my Bachelor's exam.

Prof. Anwar Kazim, however, was the most interesting of them all. Tall and skinny, he had a peculiar style of teaching: he would move his body parts a lot, like today's hosts of TV shows. He would constantly stroll from one end of the room to the other, turning and twisting his legs and squeezing his hands and shrugging his shoulders. No wonder we sometimes concentrated more on his physical movements than on comprehension and vocabulary that he taught us. Yet, we liked him very much for his jolliness and friendly manners.

Learning to Shoot, Just in Case

An exciting feature of college life was the basic military training we would receive once a week. It was called the National Cadet Corps or NCC. Students who completed the training and passed a written test and a practical demo subsequently were entitled to twenty marks to be added to their final exam total. This helped the students on the borderline of the merit list to become eligible for admission to professional colleges.

One of my class fellows, Qamar-ul-Islam Siddiqui, a very short fellow who wore thick glasses and a cheap muffler and parted his permanently oily hair in the middle, had a serious problem gripping the gun while shooting. On the day of the demo at the firing range, when his turn came to pull the trigger, he messed it up so much that the bullets went flying in all directions. It was an extremely dangerous situation, and for a moment we all thought that a real war had broken out and the end of the world was near. Thank God, a vigilant supervisor quickly put a lid on Qamar's shooting spree and saved all of us from extinction. It was a close call indeed.

Chasing Our Dreams

In 1983, SNJ and I passed the first year final exam in the first division. That wasn't good enough, though, and we vowed to do better in the second year. Unfortunately, the second year was no better than the first. As a result, neither of us was able to make it to a professional college. Father's dreams had just fallen apart.

It wasn't the end of the road, though. We could still enroll in a Bachelor's course in sciences, which we did despite our depleting confidence and interest. Luckily, F.G. College for Men also offered BSc programs and preferred its own students to those from other colleges. Seizing the favor, I enrolled in a course combination of botany, zoology, and chemistry, while SNJ embraced double maths and physics.

We both managed to pass the BSc final exams two years later, in 1986. A BSc degree meant that I could study chemistry for my Master's degree. Zoology and botany were terribly unexciting to me; nobody but me knew how I had tolerated them for two long years!

The only university of repute in Islamabad that offered chemistry was, and still is, Quaid-i-Azam University. Getting accepted there was an uphill task, for I didn't have a brilliant academic record to boast of. No wonder my application ended up in the wastepaper basket.

SNJ too was an ounce or two short of luck that year, and he drifted away from the math and physics he had worked so hard to grasp. This brought him into contact with a budding new world of computers. Encouraged by Father, SNJ enrolled himself at a private institute in Islamabad to learn the common machine languages, Basic and Fortran.

About this time, the Ministry of Defence announced some vacant posts for research assistants. Having worked for the ministry for so many years, Father knew the employer very well and asked SNJ to try. SNJ responded positively and applied for a BPS-11 post. He was selected. Although the position didn't promise a great deal of wealth or speedy promotion, it was a permanent government job, something that is intensely sought by jobseekers. Thus began SNJ's long career in public service, which continues to this day with considerable improvement in rank and remuneration.

On the other hand, I had to wait for a full year before I could apply for admission to a Master's program. It was a long and needless wait that ended in 1988 when Father encouraged me to apply to the MA English Literature program of Government College, Asghar Mall, Rawalpindi. I passed a written test and was placed on the waiting list. Luckily some successful candidates opted for other institutions, which created space for me and a few other borderline cases on the final list. Surprisingly, at no point in the admission process did it occur to me that I had taken a complete U-turn from sciences to literature.

 # Brothers and Sisters

HAVING A LARGE FAMILY WAS THE norm in the days of our grandparents and parents, when couples with more children were viewed with a lot of respect and veneration. Not just the parents themselves but also their relatives took great pride in it. However, there were also those who made fun of the large size of a family and judged it as rustic and uncivilized. Although our family of thirteen—six brothers, five sisters, and parents—was never victimized or scorned for being large, we did occasionally receive interesting comments from friends and acquaintances. One such comment was made by our outspoken arts teacher, Sir Shaukat, who wanted to know the size of our family. To my reply, "We are six brothers and five sisters," he exclaimed, "Oh my God, it's a cricket team!"

Syed Ashraf Jamil (SAJ)

A medical doctor by profession, Dr. Syed Ashraf Jamil is our eldest brother; we call him Bhaiya. He immigrated to the United States more than twenty years ago and has been settled there ever since.

Stories of Bhaiya's devotion to learning and pursuit of excellence have been told and retold by Mother. One of her oft-repeated comments is enough proof of his diligence: "When he was a medical student he would utter parts of his memorized notes while fast asleep."

After completing his MBBS from King Edward Medical College, Lahore, Bhaiya worked as a Demonstrator at Rawalpindi Medical College (RMC), Rawalpindi. He served RMC for a number of years refreshing his knowledge of medicine and saving enough money for higher education and a better job in the United States. Once there, he completed his residency in internal medicine and passed the American board. He is currently practicing as a specialist in infectious diseases in a well-known hospital in New York.

Bhaiya likes reading and keeps himself current on national and international issues and developments. He believes in playing it safe without taking undue risks. He knows a lot about technology but avoids benefiting from it unless there is a pressing need. He supports the family financially.

Syed Khalid Jamil (SKJ)

The second joy of our parents, SKJ, or Manghlay Bhai, received his B.Com. from S.M. Commerce College, Karachi, in 1975. His lucky break was a job at the Ministry of Defence, Muscat, Oman, where he worked for almost ten years making good money and gaining valuable experience.

SKJ recounts his school days as follows:

We [SKJ and STJ] were really disappointed that we had done poorly in the matriculation exam, passing it in the third division. We desperately wanted to forget it as soon as possible and move on, but we couldn't forget P-6 and P-7, our roll numbers. Secondly, without even waiting for our certificates, Father made us join a commercial institute in Raja Bazaar, Rawalpindi, where we did our C.Com & D.Com. Frankly, I passed the final exams with the help of STJ and Sir Farooqi. Things would have been dismally different had Sir Farooqi not come to our rescue.

With a D.Com degree to boast of, STJ and I set out to do our B.Com in Lahore and Karachi respectively. What is most incredible is that I was the only student at Jinnah Courts Muslim Hostel, Karachi, who was able to pass all the B.Com courses in the very first attempt! I still can't believe that such a mediocre student as I was able to achieve something as impossible as that. It still sounds like a fairy tale that I was one of the thirteen students who were declared successful.

It was about this time that I received a job offer from the Ministry of Communication, which I gladly accepted; I worked there for about four years. All credit goes to Father for making it happen.

I then enrolled in the L.L.B course at S.M. Law College, Karachi, where I was about to appear in the first year exam when a job offer from Heavy Foundry and Forge, Taxila, altered my plans. The prospect of a monthly income and the proximity of the workplace to home encouraged me to accept the offer.

In Taxila I worked for about ten months. Then, luckily, I got a job offer from the Ministry of Defence, Oman, for which all the credit again goes to Father. I worked there for ten years, from January 1, 1978, to June 30, 1988. Upon return, I joined Dolmen Group, a premier Karachi-based real estate developer and builder, and I have been working here as finance manager since 1998.

SKJ is married to Zarrin, and the two are happily settled in Karachi along with their sons, Zaid Bin Khalid and Faiz Bin Khalid. The boys are currently enrolled in MBA and CA, respectively.

Syed Tariq Jamil (STJ)

A chartered accountant by profession, STJ partners Ernst & Young Ford Rhodes Sidat Hyder, a member of the Ernst & Young Global Limited, a leading global accounting firm. He is currently a member of the executive board of the firm and office managing partner at the Islamabad office of the firm.

STJ received his B.Com in 1976 from the prestigious Hailey College of Commerce, Lahore. In January 1980, he passed the formidable CA examination, to the great joy of the family. He joined Ernst & Young in July 1982 and has been associated with it since then. Prior to this, he worked for a year as resident manager at Riaz Ahmed and Co., an accounting firm based in Rawalpindi, and for a year and a half as CFO and board member of National Film Development Corporation (NAFDEC).

STJ, or Sanghlay Bhai, is married to Raana, and the two are happily settled in Islamabad along with their daughters Maryam Tariq and Muniba Tariq.

Maryam graduated as medical doctor from Shifa College of Medicine, Islamabad, in December 2010. She is currently seeking residency in a hospital in the United States. Maryam is married to a civil engineer settled in Florida.

Muniba graduated from School of Business, Cardiff University, Wales, in July 2010, with major in marketing. She is currently working in a real estate law firm in Cardiff on a post-study visa and intends to prolong her stay in the United Kingdom for a one-year Master's program in early 2012.

Musarrat Azam

Our eldest sister, known as Baji, is a graduate of Punjab University. She is married to Ali Azam, son of Late Ali Akhtar of Sharfuddinpur, Patna, who is our maternal uncle. Azam bhai, who did his post-graduation work at Karachi University in 1983, is currently associated with National Bank of Pakistan as assistant vice president.

Baji and Azam bhai are happily settled in Islamabad along with their three children: Arsalan Ali, Asad Ali Azam, and Sundas Ali. Arsalan has completed his MBA (Finance) from International Islamic University, Islamabad. Sundas is a fourth year MBBS student of Rawalpindi Medical College, Rawalpindi, and Asad is in the second year of his post-secondary studies.

Rifat Jamil

We call her Aapa and she is, without doubt, the most diligent of our sisters: she looks after Mother twenty-four hours a day. Aapa also does most of the cooking at home and never tires of serving guests and caring for visiting family kids.

Aapa has BA and B.Ed degrees. She likes reading books and watching television. She is the most confident of our sisters.

Talat Shahbaz

Talat has BSc and B.Ed degrees from Punjab University. She worked as a science teacher at The Play School, Islamabad, from October 1990 to March 1999, before getting married to Shahbaz Ahmed, son of Late Mohammad Mashhoodul Haque, originally from Patna, Bihar.

Shahbaz is currently serving the Canadian Bar Association as its senior accountant. Prior to this, from 2006 to 2010, he worked as manager of accounts and logistics for Emircom, a UAE-based telecom concern. Earlier, Shahbaz worked for almost ten years for Greenstar Social Marketing, a large nonprofit organization providing healthcare services and products all across Pakistan.

In March 2010, the two moved to Vancouver, British Columbia, along with their daughter Mahroo Shahbaz. Mahroo is presently a Grade 5 student in a Langley school.

Syed Nasir Jamil (SNJ)

A graduate of Punjab University, SNJ knows more about computer software and electronic devices than any other family member. He is presently working as research officer in a premier research organization.

Nasir is married to Seema, daughter of Late Mohammad Mashhoodul Haque. Seema has a Master's degree in mathematics from Quaid-i-Azam University, Islamabad. She teaches mathematics at a local school.

The two are joyfully settled in Islamabad along with their sons Syed Abdullah Nasir and Syed Sabih Nasir, who are enrolled in Class 5 and Class 3, respectively.

Farhat Waheed

Farhat has BA and CT degrees from Punjab University. She is married to Syed Waheed-ud-din, son of Late Syed Alla-ud-din Mobarak, originally from Delhi, India, who later migrated to Bahawalpur, Pakistan.

Waheed bhai is an electrical engineer and is currently posted at Radio Pakistan, Islamabad. They have a daughter, Rida Waheed, and a son, Syed Aashir Waheed. Rida and Aashir are currently pursuing their post-secondary studies.

Syed Sabir Jamil (SSJ)

After receiving my Master's in English literature from Punjab University, I completed a diploma in comprehensive writing from The Writing School, Singapore. My diverse career includes my work as a journalist, advertising professional, and English teacher.

I am married to Naureen, daughter of Syed Ali Siddiqi, a former employee of Pakistan Telecommunication Company Limited.

I moved to Vancouver, British Columbia, in April 2005. We have a four-year-old daughter, Ayesha Jamil.

Shahina Jamil

The youngest of our sisters, Shahina has a Master's degree in English literature from Punjab University and a B.Ed from AIOU Islamabad. Soon after completing her MA, Shahina joined a local school as an English teacher and has been associated with teaching ever since.

Shahina likes to read books and watch television plays. She also likes cooking and does so occasionally.

Syed Tahir Jamil

The youngest member of our family, Tahir passed his FSc (premedical) from Sir Syed College, Rawalpindi, in the First Division. Then he got himself enrolled in the MBBS program at the Quaid-i-Azam Medical College, Bahawalpur. However, due to ill health, Tahir could not continue his medical education and had to forgo it soon after passing the second professional exam. Later, Tahir joined a local medical transcription company by the name of C'soft and worked there for a few months before joining two other MT firms.

 # Father's Illness and Exit

FATHER HAD HIS FIRST HEALTH WARNING about twenty years before he fell critically ill. A mild heart attack had spilled the tea he was sipping in the drawing room of our F-8/1 residence. SAJ and STJ were quick to take him to the nearest hospital. The doctor prescribed him pills for the heart and blood pressure that he would take for the rest of his life. The doctor also advised him to cut down on his salt intake and do some lifestyle changes.

Father always took the doctor's advice seriously; his blood pressure would rise every now and then, but without sounding any real alarm. He continued to perform his everyday duties, like visiting *masjid* for the obligatory prayers, managing utility bills, reading the morning newspaper, and occasionally watching cricket, hockey, and wrestling on TV. An occasional visit by Azizi sahib or Syed sahib or a son or a son-in-law made his day. Father also visited them every so often.

Things started to get worse in 2001, when Father was diagnosed with a malignant prostate. He was almost eighty then, which meant that a surgical procedure was out of the question. The doctors at Aga Khan Hospital in Karachi, who first broke the shocking news, were furious to learn that none of the physicians in Islamabad, who had seen Father a number of times, had the good sense to get the simple PSA test done, which could have led to early detection and possible treatment of the illness.

Father's blood pressure and ailing heart were now not as much a matter of concern as his malignant prostate. With surgery ruled out for reasons of old age, the only thing they could offer was painkillers.

But painkillers kill pain, not the source of pain. The temporary relief that the painkillers provided didn't improve Father's condition at all. As a result, he started losing vigor and energy, but not hope! It was hope that kept him going. The best thing he could do in such a painful situation was sleep as much as he could, which wasn't always possible in view of the endless pain in his legs. Whenever he went to sleep, we made sure that he slept for as much time as possible.

While each family member played his or her part in looking after Father, STJ's role was the most commendable. Despite his hectic work schedule and professional commitments, he always kept himself available for Father for everything, from driving him to hospitals to buying pills and injections and drips. It was an excellent example of time and money well spent. Equally praiseworthy was SAJ's continuous monetary support through those painful times.

Nobody lives forever. This bitter truth dawned on us on May 10, 2003, when Father breathed his last. His was a peaceful exit. Death proved to be the most effective painkiller for him.

Numbers Do Matter, Don't They?

A careful study of the important dates in Father's life, carried out by STJ, reveals a recurring pattern of 4 and 8. Take a look at these.

- Father was born on 10/7/1922, which totals 4 (1+0+7+1+9+2+2=22=2+2=4)

- Father had two brothers and a sister (all departed), so including him the total again is 4.

- Father's sister Roqaiya Khatoon was married in 1939 (1+9+3+9=22=4).

- It was in 1939 (1+9+3+9=22=4) that Father added "Dighvi" to his name, which remained his better-known name for many years.

- Father passed his matriculation exam in 1939 (1+9+3+9=22=4).

- His trip to Calcutta and the Second World War, a significant event to which he had been a witness, started in 1939 (1+9+3+9=22=4).

- Father was married on the twenty-second day, which totals 4 (2+2).

- Father migrated to East Pakistan on the thirteenth day, which again represents 4 (1+3).

- His first child, Syed Ashraf Jamil, was born on May 8, 1952, at 5:30 p.m. The day is 8, the total of the year is 8 (1+9+5+2=17=8); the total of time is 8 (5+3+0=8)

- Father joined the Ministry of Defence, Rawalpindi, in 1970, the total of which is 8 (1+9+7+0=17=8).

- The total number of his family members is 13 (2 parents + 11 children), which again totals 4.

- The number allotted to his first house built in Magh Bazaar, Dhaka, was 521, the total of which is 8 (5+2+1).

- The number allotted to his second house in Mohammadpur, Dhaka, was 26, the total of which is 8 (2+6).

- The number of his first residence in Islamabad was 17, the total of which is 8 (1+7), and the sector in which this house was located is F-8.

- The street in sector G-10/1 where he built his house after retirement is 8, and the house number was 444.

- The number of the house where he last resided is 715, the total of which is 4 (7+1+5=13=1+3=4).

- The hospital where he breathed his last, PIMS, is situated in sector G-8.

- The plot number of his grave is 17, the total of which is 8 (1+7), and the graveyard is in sector H-8.

- The project ID of this book based on his life is 370066, which again is a total of 4. The project was given to the publisher in 2011, the total of which is 4.

Father's Fortitude and Austerity Code

One of Father's greatest possessions was his endless stock of patience and hope. Without it, he would never have succeeded in raising eleven children and helping them stand on their own feet.

A government employee who mostly performed his duties as a Grade-17 section officer, Father must have endlessly enjoyed the special blessings of God Almighty, for nothing else can explain how his meager monthly salary, about two thousand rupees for most part of his career, could feed, clothe, house, and educate six sons and five daughters. It was nothing but the refreshing energy of his beliefs that kept his torch of hope burning. Not once did we find him irritable or complaining.

However, it was not just his unshakable conviction that kept him going; he was also immensely practical in approach and prudent in using resources. Austerity, for example, was one of his golden principles. "Never waste a thing that you can reuse in the future," he would tell us. Used clothes were not to be thrown away; they were never out of fashion. Also, there was no shame in younger siblings wearing the used clothes of their older brothers and sisters.

Father would never buy expensive stuff from large sparkling superstores if the same could be purchased at much cheaper prices at ordinary shops. He would not hesitate to buy our school uniforms at the economical Lunda Bazaar, the hub of second-hand clothes in Rawalpindi. He would cheer us up with a credible justification: "In winter we need warm clothes, not new ones; the whole idea is to protect ourselves from the bitter cold so that we don't fall sick." We occasionally challenged Father's logic, but our impulsive arguments were always defeated by his sound reasoning. It was impossible to outwit him on principles.

Austerity didn't mean that we could not wear new clothes at all. Father would still buy us brand new clothes from time to time. He would make sure that each one of us wore new *shalwar kameez* on Eid days. To save some money, Father would get them tailored, as ready-made dresses are always more expensive.

Father would spend the money thus saved not on his own development, but on feeding us and paying our tuition fees and buying our school stationery. Hence, like other children, we never had fewer than three meals a day, never slept hungry, were never kicked out of school for nonpayment of fees, and were never short of notebooks or textbooks. Although as long as Father supported us singlehandedly, we didn't have the luxury of enjoying meat or fish or chicken every day, we never had the feeling that we were being neglected or unfairly treated. We enjoyed meat and chicken occasionally and fish rarely, and whenever distant relatives visited us once or twice a year, we always picked up our share in the sumptuous dinners cooked primarily for the guests.

Possessions and Belongings

Father's austerity code applied not only to food and clothing but also to household items like furniture and kitchenware. Our first sofa set, for example, was a green eighteenth-century couch without arms. Just because it had a set of springs, it was called a sofa. It was perhaps the weirdest thing in the spacious drawing room of our 20-A/1 residence.

Secondly, the plywood dining table was so big that it was used as a makeshift bed by SAJ when he was still a medical student. Father couldn't afford another bed, or the house just didn't have enough space for another piece of furniture. Later, when we moved from our 20-A/1 residence to less roomy accommodations in Rawalpindi, Father summoned a carpenter and made him slash the sides and the legs of the dining table to half its original size. The shortened form was then used only as a dining table. And when we moved to our G-11/1 house, our present residence, we replaced it with a brand new dining table, finer and broader than the old one, to match the splendor of the new dwelling. We dispatched the old one upstairs to be used as a dumping ground for old books and miscellaneous household stuff.

Similarly, many of the kitchen tools and dishes that were bought by Father from time to time or were given to Mother as wedding gifts by her parents are still in our possession. These include the big round silver trays or *saenis*, which were used in the past and are still used sometimes to spread the many varieties of *halwa*—*suji*, *besun*, *daal*, etc., cooked on the holy occasion of *Shab-e-Baraat*.

We also had a medium bronze *deghchi* occasionally used to cook a special dish like *pulao* or *biryani*. It was probably donated to a *naukarani* (maid) or was lost when we moved from Rawalpindi to Islamabad.

The most elegant of the antiques that we still possess is a silver *ittar daan* (perfume holder), more noticeable on Eid days. On Eid eve, Father would get it cleaned and adorn it with two tiny *ittar* (natural, nonalcoholic perfume) bottles (*sheshi*) bought a day or two before Eid. It is customary to apply the *ittar* to our hands and clothes before leaving home for the Eid prayers. Those who visited us on Eid days were also offered the *ittar;* the typical scent of the *ittar* added to the joy of the festivities.

During the annual *Milaad* meetings held to commemorate the birthday of Prophet Muhammad (upon whom be peace and blessings of Allah) two silver vases with perforated tops were used to sprinkle rosewater on the assembly just before the end of the recitations, when the participants would stand up to conclude the ritual. These meetings used to be held at our place for a number of years before Father stopped holding them.

We also had a bronze *badhna* (water container) for washroom use. It had served us for twenty odd years when it was ultimately replaced by a plastic *lota*. The plastic *lota* is lighter in weight, easier to use, and a lot cheaper, but less durable than its bronze ancestor.

We also possessed an old portable kerosene lantern, *laaltan*, that helped us see things during the occasional power breakdowns. It went out of fashion as soon as candles were introduced as an alternative.

We also had a flat, five-sided stone, fifteen inches by ten inches, called *sill*. It came with a small triangular stone called *batta*. The *sill-batta*, a permanent feature of the kitchen those days, was used to crush garlic flakes, coriander, mint leaves, and some other spices to make chutney. For well over fifty years, Mother used the *sill-batta* to grind the herbs. She crushed them so skillfully that there was no wastage at all: none of the ground spices ever spilled over the *sill*. The *sill-batta* was replaced by an electric grinder in 1980.

Father's Character and Moral Principles

Father, without doubt, was morally sound with a spotless character. Worldly charms and temptations never derailed him. He neither abused anyone nor let anyone abuse him. There were very few occasions when he lost temper; however, he never used foul language to vent his anger.

Above all, Father kept a fine balance between religious and secular inclinations. Being a born moderate, he endorsed both as equally important. He never missed his obligatory prayers. Even in cold winter nights, when the other family members slept comfortably in their cozy beds, he would wake up in time to catch the *jamaat* (assembly) for *Fajr* (predawn) prayers. He would fast the whole month of Ramadan. More than once, he even lodged himself in a local mosque for *aetekaaf*, the spiritual retreat in the last ten days of Ramadan.

On the secular front, Father would never hesitate to carry out his everyday tasks, the purely temporal ones that benefited himself and his family. He would dress up like an officer and wear a three-piece suit to work every morning and to parties occasionally. He would see to it that we dressed neatly and polished our shoes and combed our hair before leaving for school or work.

Although domestic engagements consumed much of Father's time—looking after eleven children wasn't easy—he would never think twice when it came to helping kith and kin and friends and neighbors who sought his help and advice from time to time. He would occasionally send some money, out of his limited income, to his not-so-affluent sister Roqaiya Khatoon in India, with whom he corresponded quite regularly. (Roqaiya Khatoon, our *phupee*, passed away in India a few years ago). Father would give out a portion of his *Zakat* (Muslim charity) to a local cobbler who mended his shoes. When the cobbler died, Father did not withdraw his support but started supporting the cobbler's son.

In another instance, upon learning that the elderly mother of the local *imam masjid* had cramps, Father got her examined free of cost by SAJ, a medical doctor by then, at our F-8/1 residence. On another occasion, Father cheerfully lent his wooden *chowke* (low table) to the imam of our mosque when he needed something to stand on to deliver the Eid sermon in the children's park adjacent to our house in G-10/1.

Indeed, Father's high moral standards constituted the hallmark of his personality.

 # A Tireless Mother

SINCE THE TIME WE FIRST BECAME conscious of the protective presence of Mother, we haven't found her idle or uncaring even for a single moment. It is hard, almost impossible, to find a word or a phrase that can adequately describe the amount of love and affection Mother has showered on us all these long years and the selfless and endless hard work she has done every single day to feed us, to clothe us, and to protect us from the wickedness of people and the perils of nature.

Giving birth to eleven children delivered a year or two apart in itself is a great achievement, which speaks volumes for her amazing emotional, mental, and physical capacity. Not many genes blossom into mothers as motherly as ours!

When we were still very young and immature, unable to comprehend the complexities of life, we hardly realized how one person we called Mother could do all the things she would do to keep us safe and secure; how she would wake up in time to cook sizzling breakfast for all of us, a family of thirteen, to make certain that we didn't go to school or work hungry; how she would keep our school uniforms neat and clean and pressed for us to wear every single weekday; how she would keep lunch ready for us when we returned from school; how she wouldn't go to bed until we all returned from work, sometimes very late at night; how in the middle of frosty nights she would willingly ruin her own sweet sleep to walk to our beds to make sure that our blankets properly covered us, and that we slept tight; how, when we fell sick, she would nurse us, prepare stomach-friendly food for us, and see to it that we took the bitter pills the doctor prescribed us; how, one afternoon, when she had nothing to cook for lunch, she plucked the leaves of a spinach-like vegetable growing in our 20-A/1 backyard, to make food; how, on the eve of Eid, while fixing Father's Eid suit, she accidentally pierced her fingertip under the sewing machine needle, and that really hurt her; and how, one day, when I was crying my eyes out for a ten-paisa coin, she pleaded a family member to lend her the coin to pacify me. The list is endless.

Mother's unconditional support to Father all the fifty-plus years of their coexistence is, without doubt, her greatest achievement. It included such daunting tasks as embracing Father's serious disposition and temperament, abiding by his strict code of conduct, and learning to live within his financial boundaries.

And what a prudent companion she was, using her husband's meager resources with tons of care and caution without ever letting us feel the tremendous hardship he went through every single day to make both ends meet. It wasn't easy, I can tell you! It wasn't easy! Without her good sense, endless patience, and endurance in the face of hardships, the family could never have progressed and prospered the way it eventually did. It wasn't easy!

How was Mother able to accomplish this daunting task? With the strength of her belief in God, her infinite energy of hope, and her resolute commitment to duty. Nursing a whole lot of dependent children (each one more demanding than the other), feeding and clothing them, taking care of them in times of joy and in times of distress, and dealing with a matter-of-fact husband at the same time are no minor achievements. What else does one expect from a mother? May she live forever for all of us!